How I Found My Peace

How I Found My Peace

AN OFFER OF HOPE TO THOSE MAINTAINING SOBRIETY IN THE MIDST OF DYSFUNCTION

A MEMOIR BY
RACHEL CLARK

To request permission, contact the author at:
        raerae623@aol.com

ISBN: 978-1-958150-06-1
How I Found My Peace: An offer of hope to those maintaining sobriety in the midst of dysfunction
A memoir by Rachel Clark

Paperpack
September 2022

Subjects:
SELF-HELP / Substance Abuse & Addictions / Alcohol
BIOGRAPHY & AUTOBIOGRAPHY / Personal Memoirs
FAMILY & RELATIONSHIPS / General

Cover Photo by Dean Clark

Tomorrow

The love of God has hung a veil
Around tomorrow,
That we may not its beauty see,
Nor trouble borrow.

But, oh, 'tis sweeter far to trust
His unseen hand
And know that all the path of life
His wisdom planned.

I know not if tomorrow's way
Be steep or rough,
But when His hand is guiding me,
This is enough.

And so, although the veil has hid
Tomorrow's way,
I walk with perfect faith and trust
Through each today

~ Bertha H. Pentney
from her book _Songs of a Servant_

Women of Jeep

Women of Jeep, your friendship has meant the world to me. My life was made better because you were in it. I love you and I appreciate all the times you've been there for me.

You are all some very strong women and great examples of what it takes to nurture and work and provide all at the same time. I know some of the sacrifices you've all made for the love of family.

Angelina Garcia - Williamson

Ursula Soto

Jackie Rodriguez

Chris Villegas Romo and sister

Marie Villagas

Ruth Duvall

Vera Manuel Salser Henrick

Pat Strong

Kimberly Vining - Bell

Jackie Barnes

Cathy Robles Gonzalas

Denise Jackson

Terri Tracy

Beverly Marsh

Cheryl Coffman

Cheryl Greenburg

Deb Ruthenberg

Joan Bell Limmer

Karen Cantu you can do this!

Lisa Smith

Maggie Mattox

Marcia Sweeney - Young

Cheri Hauser

Marie Craft

Mary Lou Wortring

Mee Sanders

Suzie Dudley

Tina Kerr - Wheeler

Tina Peart

Vickie Marino

Zacchi Pollard

Michele Breeden

Rose Woodward

Bobbie McCullough and
   daughter Dalina Marinski

Warm thanks to Special Friends ~

Dena Foreman

Susan McClain Good

Cheryl - Emm Liebich

Cindy Gregg

Janice Dean Grimes

In Memory ~

Marsha A Loboschefski

Paul D Rodriguez

Julian C Zapata

TABLE OF CONTENTS

Matriach of the family Angelina Rocha Garcia with Benjamin Garcia
and daughters Esperanza and Catalina

INTRODUCTION

I was born into a migrant family in Ohio six decades ago. My mom Rosa and her siblings (two sisters and three brothers), along with parents Benjamin and Angelina crossed the border from Mexico into Mercedes, Texas, when Rosa was just five years old. Papa, the patriarch of the family, had ridden with Francisco Pancho Villa during the Mexican Revolution. Ama, the matriarch, was an *adelita* (woman soldier) who also fought during the Mexican Revolution even though men didn't like women on the battlefield. Ama's family went north following work through the states before settling in Toledo, Ohio, and found work in the fields picking tomatoes and in the greenhouses planting petunias. They were a close knit family, working, drinking, playing, and singing their Spanish music together.

Rosa was a binge drinker, and at times would leave me and my little brother Scottie at home alone for days at a time. This story is about how I've tried to navigate my life based upon my upbringing and things I thought to be the norm that were actually very dysfunctional. I'm telling the story of what it was like being raised in a traditional Catholic, Spanish-speaking home with very strict rules and how alcohol impacted many parts of my life along the way.

You'll read about my struggle to understand the dynamics within my family growing up, along the way turning to alcohol myself. Then ultimately finding the courage to change.

Nearly three decades ago I set out to make changes. Albeit not in a manner that I would recommend for anyone else, but my will was strong and I did it the only way I knew how. Through my struggles I learned many lessons and want to share them with you, so that you may have hope as well and know that any changes, be it ever so small, can make huge differences in the future.

But you have to want change and it's not an easy thing to do most times. Whether it's drinking or being in a bad relationship. If happiness is what you want in life, it's worth going after.

Throughout my journey I've learned just how important it is to have a toolbox in times of crisis. My crisis was alcohol and a dysfunctional marriage, brought on by years and years of neglect and feelings of hurt and loneliness, guilt and shame, and a myriad of other things. I know I'm not alone and there are others who suffer as I did as well. I've learned that drinking often ends up with people being combative and easily agitated, and my toolbox has helped me to be hopeful in these situations.

For years I had in the back of my mind to write a book, but I never knew what it would be about or even if it was a possibility for me. But then one day, scrolling through TikTok, that all changed. One video caught my attention. The video isn't important to describe, but when the narrator said, "Today. At this moment, if you're watching this, this is your wake up call... Do not take what God put in you to the grave with you." I listened. I woke up.

As she said it, it clicked with me – there are things that only you were created to do. Sometimes it's scary to go into unfamiliar territory, it's hard to imagine how you're going to find time to write the book. How you're going to find the resources to start the business.

She said that the first step I needed to take, yes me, because I felt as if she was speaking to me directly was that I needed to write the vision down! Which I did not do, but I did purpose it in my heart that I needed to write my story, it would not go to the grave with me.

How was I going to do this? I'm barely educated I thought? To which I answered, one story at a time.

And the stories starting flowing out, one at a time. Each one shares a part of what I went through in an effort not only for me to understand how I made it to River Road in the first place, and also to share what I learned in hopes that it will help you on your journey to YOUR River Road.

The TikTok video that inspired this book:
https://www.tiktok.com/@fitspossibletrucking/
video/7036126605504417070

A view of River Road

Making My Way To River Road

As a teenager I'd never been down River Road, not until Bill Davis loaded us up in his car one evening, Mom, myself, Angie, and Scott to take a ride and look at Christmas lights – I'd never seen so many.

The houses were mansions compared to the two bedroom bungalow we lived in. The Christmas lights glistened against the white snow and shined more beautifully than anything I'd ever seen before. We didn't have any lights. We were lucky to have a Christmas tree. From the car we could see big beautiful decorations all around the houses and even the porches and in the large picture windows featured perfectly decorated trees against the night.

I remember thinking that one day I would love to live on River Road. The full road of River Road stretches from Toledo (just past the Toledo Zoo) and winds up along the Maumee River – up past Grand Rapids, Ohio, and continues many more miles into Indiana.

When it came time to build our new home, Dean and I settled on an affordable piece of land, with a little over five acres, on State Route 24 – now known as South River Road. We wanted to move out in the country to raise the kids. City life in Toledo was beginning to get bad. The older kids had already had their bikes stolen right from our yard. Crime overall in Toledo was increasing.

It wasn't long after we moved in that we heard on the news that a new bypass was going to be built in our area. We thought it couldn't come fast enough. The truck traffic on the otherwise rural road made things very dangerous, even more so at night after you throw deer into the mix.

I laid in bed one night thinking, "Well if Mrs. Wagner can do it, if she can travel on this road daily with all the truck traffic, I guess I can too..." After all, they were our neighbors and have been living in their home for 10 years.

We had no idea about the truck traffic until after we purchased the land and were making regular trips to see the progress on the home being built.

It was downright scary just pulling into the driveway if you had a trucker on your ass. You had to turn on your blinker a mile down the road, well maybe not quite a mile but you had to give a good notice that you'd be turning into your driveway well in advance so that they could have ample time to apply the brakes. It's just a two lane highway. After the bypass was built they renamed our road to South River Road. So in a roundabout kinda way I did finally make it to River Road. It is a country living at its best, just five miles outside of Waterville, Ohio, where you can get groceries at Kroger or ice cream at Sweet Retreat. We even have a public library and an excellent mexican restaurant, La Cocina De Carlos.

But anyway.... that's the road I'm on and next up are the stories that got me here, one by one.

Mom and Phillip Greenwood

The story I was told is that Mom was 19 when she married Robert Friesner. Not much is known about their marriage. What we do know is that it was very short. I think they moved to another state briefly and separated a little later, which is when Mom met and had an affair with another man and I was a product of that affair. I don't know if she didn't know whose baby I was because of the time frame, or she didn't want to have to tell Robert Friesner that I wasn't his at the time, or what. But she had many people scratching their heads for many years. One of Robert Friesner's sisters through the years would bring me Christmas presents from his mom, who I knew as Grandma Friesner, though I had never met her. I would come to meet her years later.

I was four years old when Mom married Phillip Greenwood. Together in 1968 they had my brother Scott Vincent; he is seven years younger than me. Shortly thereafter they lost a baby boy to stillbirth who they named Christopher.

That marriage was pretty short as well, and ended in divorce in 1972. I think it had a lot to do with the drinking and fighting that was always going on. No one living today knows how or where Mom met Phillip. I asked everyone. It is one of the biggest regrets I have to this day, not asking more questions while my mom was still alive. There is so much I don't know. I don't know how she met the man who turned out to be my father. But then I'm getting a little ahead of myself... more on that subject later.

Drinking was a big thing in the family, all my *tios* (uncles) and *tias* (aunts) like to party and have a good time. Tio Pancho was a guitarist and played on a Mexican radio station, although a few others played as well – he was the main one and the others would join in with the singing. Tio Pancho had the best Mexican *grito* (shout) as any I've ever heard to this day, followed only by my Tia Lupe.

The Mexican *grito* often accompanies celebrations, mariachi music, and is part of a national celebration every September 16. It is more of a loud yell – it is an expression of excitement, joy, and pride in the Mexican communities.

They had such beautiful voices – I can still hear them in memory. But along with that partying, singing, dancing, and beer drinking came many arguments.

They liked to hang out in the several neighborhood taverns as they were called in those days and there were quite a few in the area of South and Broadway in Toledo, Ohio, as I can remember and as kids we were in and out of them as well right along with them. Except for when Tia Catita lived across the street from one on Segur Avenue, it was called the Drop Inn and they could leave us at the house and go right across the street. How convenient, right? On occasion a brawl would break out and sometimes it even involved the family.

I remember being little and crying because my stepdad Phillip was banging on the door drunk wanting to be let in and Mom and Tia Catita would not let him in, they were telling him to go away.

Another time at the Drop Inn, when I was four or five years old, I was sitting with my mom at a table, I don't remember who else was there when the fight broke out, but I do remember Mom having to pull Tia Lupe into the bathroom along with the bar stool she was sitting on because her cowboy boot was wedged around the frame and stuck.

Just this afternoon I was thinking to myself, is it possible that I can recall such things from such a young age? Because I can recall bits and pieces from as early as four years old. And Google said yes, it is even possible to have memories from the age of two and a half. That is astounding to me.

Mom and Phillip's first home after they got married was a trailer in a trailer park in the area of North Detroit Avenue and Glendale; just up the street about a block was another tavern called The Ding Dong that my mom would frequent with one of her friends from the trailer park. A younger woman, Yolanda, who I believe was also Mexican from Laredo, Texas, together with my mom took turns carrying me through the snow to go to The Ding Dong after Phillip left for work.

He worked second shift at Devilbiss, a tool and die company in Toledo. Mom would go to The Ding Dong and then rush home just before Phillip was expected and in a hurry put me to bed and his pot pies in the oven – he lived off of those things.

She liked the Ding Dong because they had a man in there who played the piano and he would let her sing her favorite song Blue Moon. I would curl up in the booth and fall asleep and she would cover me with the coats. I remember them laughing and stumbling home taking turns carrying me.

I swore I would never live in a trailer after one caught fire in the park and the owner was on our doorstep in his underwear asking for help.

At five we moved into our first home. We moved to a one story bungalow. Every room in the house could be seen from every room in the house. We had a mirror in the living room that ran the length of the sofa and was about four feet high. It took up almost the whole wall and was a wedding gift from Grandma and Grandpa Greenwood when Mom married their son Phillip.

Mom loved family pictures and displayed them on the walls and on top of the television. Mom had a twin bed in her room for my brother Scott, and I had my own room. In it I had an old buffet I used to put my clothes in and on top I would line up all my dolls, just to be able to look at them. I never played with them. I just liked to look at them because I thought they were so pretty.

It was a small house but very cozy and comforting. It sat at the end of a dead end street. Behind the backyard were 12 steps that led to the creek that we would go and sit by and just listen to the flowing water. On the other side was a hill covered with brush and trees and at the top of the hill were railroad tracks.

A train would go by and the whole house would vibrate. We were surrounded by open fields. Very quiet and peaceful. That was home for the next 14 years.

There were many fights between Mom and Phillip where drinking was involved.

One night they were arguing and he threw the pink princess phone at her face and broke her nose. I was screaming and crying as I watched the blood run down her face. It was cold and snowing and I ran out of the house with no shoes on and Phillip chased me and brought me back kicking and screaming. I was trying to make it to the neighbors house to get help. He had to take her to the hospital that night to get her nose reset.

Another time they were coming back from a party at Grandma and Grandpa Greenwood's house – New Years I believe – and she slipped and fell getting out of the car on the ice and broke her leg in three parts. She had to be in a wheelchair for quite some time and my older cousin Connie would come to help her.

There came a time that Mom started going out without him and he'd do the same and caused more problems between the two especially when drinking was involved. He would get very mean and Mom liked to argue, sometimes she just wouldn't quit.

I don't know what all the arguing was about. I just remember that when they had enough and got divorced, Mom went out and bought brand new furniture, Early American, and some new tables and lamps that had wheels that actually turned. She bought a China cabinet and matching table and chairs for the dining room. All compliments of Phillip, though he knew nothing about them. The last hoorah sort of. He called her *chica* and I remember him sitting in the living room on that new couch with that toothpick in his mouth, nodding his head and laughing and telling her that it was the last bit of money she was ever going to get from him and that she better enjoy it and make it last!

Phillip was a nice looking man, a little heavy at that time, with black hair he parted to the side in a little swoop of bangs, he kept his hair at the nape of his neck and wore a beard and mustache. He didn't talk loud, but man he could cuss. He would throw son of a bitches all over the place and use the m-f- word like crazy. He would thump me on my head if I didn't move fast enough to get in or out of the door. I remember that and as a child it would hurt my feelings. I would try to duck my head because I knew it was coming.

He was a binge drinker later after the divorce. He started to take Disulfiram (Antabuse), which is used to treat alcoholics. He would take a pill every day so that he wouldn't drink. If he did drink along with the pill it could cause a myriad of reactions, such as throbbing headache, nausea, vomiting, fast and irregular heartbeat, and fainting, just to name a few. And that's how he was able to quit drinking. If he knew he wanted to drink like at income tax time or a New Year celebration he just wouldn't take his pills for a couple days. And then he would have to commit himself for three days at the Red Cross to sober up. He would call someone to come and pick him up when it was all done.

Mom was very beautiful. At four feet, 11 inches tall, she had a very thin petite figure. She would paint her eyes like a cat and wore ruby red lipstick. She had a hump on her nose and she was really proud of it and told us it was on a wooden nickel. I don't know if that's true or not. But she said it told of her Indian heritage. Her grandmother was Mestiza. A mix of Spanish and Indian. She wore her hair up a lot, teased and puffed at the top of her head, and kept it in place with the ever popular bobby pins. She had really coarse hair, and lots of it.

Mom had an eighth grade education. She was the daughter of migrant workers who crossed the border with her family from Mexico into Texas when she was just five years old. Her family had been coming back and forth to work but this time they had planned to stay.

Patriarch Benjamin Garica had a younger brother Leonardo Garcia who was already in the United States and had saved up enough money to bring the entire Garica family out of Mexico... all except for the oldest daughter, Tia Esperanza, who was married and had children and had to remain in Mexico.

Papa, Benjamin Garcia, the patriarch of the family, rode with Francisco Pancho Villa during the Mexican Revolution. A family member has the one and only photo of him during that time. He is on a horse and appears to be wearing a uniform of possibly a General.

He named his firstborn son Francisco after Villa, and we called him Tio Pancho.

Ama was only 15 when she became an orphan with a younger brother, Vicente. As the story goes, Papa took her and her brother in and cared for them both.

Mom liked to laugh and have fun, but was very quick tempered. She could easily engage in conversation on just about anything. Even if she didn't know, she would pretend to know about any subject.

Matriach of the family Angelina Rocha
Garcia and oldest daughter Esperanza

Tias and Tios

Tio Pancho, Tia Lupe, Tio Jose

Tia Catalina and oldest daughter Adeline   Benjamín García Jr

24

Tio Pancho, Ama, Rachel 2 yrs old, Gregory, Angie, and Rosa Garcia

chel age 7 with brother Scottie

My mom Rosa holding me as a baby. Angie and brother Gregory and prima Lupita Arriaga

25

THE EARLY YEARS

Mom's drinking didn't stop with the divorce from Phillip. She was now in the home collecting child support for my brother Scottie and welfare and food stamps, with a mortgage that was $61 a month – she continued purchasing the house that Phillip quitclaim deeded to her through a land contract deal.

Mom never went to work after she and Phillip married, though at one time she did have a job for just a short time working at Tidkies Department Store in downtown Toledo in the cafeteria. She would attend their reunions and often talked about a couple lady friends she made while there.

My mom very rarely drank at home unless it was her birthday or a sibling's birthday and they came to the house to drink with her. She simply didn't have the money for it. On the first of the month she liked to play bingo and had a little money to take a cab and go for a few drinks to the taverns, but then she would forget to come home.

First she got us babysitters, actually just one and her name was Wanda and she lived in the neighborhood. But after just one time of Mom not coming home like she was supposed to, Wanda's mom never let her babysit again. We woke up in the morning to find Wanda still there sleeping on the couch. She called her mom and they wondered what to do and it was sometime in the afternoon that Mom made it home and Wanda was able to go home.

After that we didn't get a babysitter and I was in charge of watching Scottie while Mom went out. I mean... I was 12 and it was the two of us. I remember watching the clock, because I knew that after she played Bingo she was going to go to the tavern and I knew what time the taverns closed. Just like to this day they closed at 2:30 AM and I would start calling the two or three that she frequented and ask to speak to her and make her promise that she was coming home right after they closed. But she never did. After the first couple times of her not coming home I would call her and cry and plead for her to come home and she always said she would but she never did. Sometimes she didn't even come the next day.

My mom was an alcoholic. She didn't drink every day and rarely drank at home, but once she got out and away and had a few drinks she just couldn't stop. She didn't until she made herself sick out there on the street, God knows with who doing what. While her children were home alone.

I wasn't scared. I was just a little girl who wanted her mom. I begged and cried to her to please come home and she would say, "I am coming home, Rachel." I made her promise and she would say one thing and do another. But she didn't come home and I would curl up on the sofa by the window and fall asleep waiting for her.

Imagine being so young and coming to the realization that it just didn't do any good to call and beg... I simply stopped calling. It became clear to me that whatever was out there was more important than what was at home.

I never went to kindergarten, and first grade was spent at St. Charles School and it was far enough away that I needed to get a ride every day. That's probably why it only lasted one year. At the time my Mom didn't drive, or have a car of her own, and she didn't work, so she would be home every day. On occasion she would work in the cafeteria passing out food.

I peed my panties in class one day because I was too afraid to ask the Nun if I could use the bathroom. We were all standing in a circle around the perimeter of the room. I remember we were holding hands and the pee just started running down my legs. The boy to one side noticed and I'm pretty sure he was the one who told everyone else. I never said a word even after the fact. The school had to call my mom to bring me a change of clothes.

When it was time to go into the second grade I was going to a new school. Walbridge Elementary was about seven blocks from where we lived on Pere Street in south Toledo and it seemed like it was so far away, because it was! Especially for a small child. I suppose we got rides in those early years because I sure as heck don't remember walking until about the fourth or fifth grade.

One day as I exited the building, there was Mom, waiting for me. She had ridden my three speed english racer bicycle that she had got for me using Top Value Stamps up to the school to surprise me. She was tired and winded and asked Howard, one of the neighborhood boys, to ride it back home and she walked with Scotti and I back home.

Mom would play the radio and hold dance contests in the front yard for the neighborhood kids. We would couple up and she was the one and only judge. She would give apples or whatever she had, sometimes baggies of popcorn she'd pop in the kitchen and fill herself, and that would be the prize. It was the simplest thing but so much fun. We would laugh and really try hard to be the best dancers to win that silly prize.

There were a couple of boys my age, we were about 12, who were always vying for my attention and I knew, even at that age, that I had an influence over them. We would have a contest to see which one I was going to like.

I would say things like, "whoever runs the fastest to that pole or whoever runs the slowest, wins!" Oh gosh, how I played those boys. They were both so cute and I really liked both Howard Mayo and Mike Lee, I would walk with them to school.

I really liked that school but Mom wasn't the best at getting me up and ready. She would yell at me from her bed to get up and I would go and curl up in front of the heater in the dining room and fall back to sleep. It was a blow heater and I can still remember how good that warm air felt on me. I was a bedwetter late in my years probably until about 10 and she would just have me come out of the wet clothes and into some dry ones. I must've smelled really good for the kids at school. Taking baths was not a priority, either. I remember taking a bath and dirt and dry skin floating on top of the water. I was so confused at the time as to what it was and tried to get away from it.

We had a dance program in the fourth grade, our teacher Mrs. Carroll had us learn four or five dances. One was a Hawaiian dance and we used actual bamboo sticks sitting on the floor knocking them together with a partner. Another was a Greek dance and we made a big circle and put our arms around each others' shoulders and we put a lot of work into it! Mom wanted me to look nice, she even bought me a new dress – a really pretty sunshine yellow color, it had a lace outer layer and the yellow dress showed underneath the lace. At the time my hair was really long and Mom tied it into a half up ponytail.

I was walking to school by myself for the program, after school hours, and I saw one of the boys in my class, Felix Blanco, though we called him Happy. Happy said to me, "why do you look so white?" To which I replied, "I took a bath." Oh, the thought of that many years later and it still horrifies me to this day. What kind of thing is that to say? But it was true and honest and I did look white with my long hair pulled back half up in a pony tail with my new yellow dress on. I was actually pretty light skinned, I earned the nickname *güera* (white girl) as a child.

The dance was so much fun and we did so well with the dances we learned. I was so proud. Throughout the years, because of that scenario in that bathtub that day, I found it very hard to sit in a tub of water. I forever let the water run and use a large cup to pour the water over myself.

To this day I have a beautiful garden tub that I've only been in two times in the last 20 years. I promised myself that that was going to change this year as I'm retired now and it's time to enjoy that tub.

Growing up I had two friends on the block – Susan and Julie. Julie was the same age as me, Susan was a couple years older. Both girls were blond and had very fair skin. Julie had one brother named Mark and Susan had a brother Mike and a sister named Marsha who were both older then Sue.

Depending on what day of the week it was they would be friends with me.

Julie had a pool that I went into one time. Mom bought me my one and only bathing suit ever to go into that pool one time! It was just unheard of as modesty was the rule. Walking out of the bathroom in a towel? Unheard of! NOBODY ever did it.

Julie also had a Barbie collection and the reason I know that is that I was invited once to play with them. Mom never bought Barbies for me, she would buy the bigger play dolls and I sometimes wonder if I was secretly envious of those Barbies my friend had and then held some kind of grudge against Barbie herself because I never bought them for my own girls years later. Like I swore some kind of allegiance against her.

Julie and Susan both had both parents at home and I remember getting rides to school with Susan. I would walk over and wait on the stoop for them to come out.

At Easter time Mom would save her eggs shells and stuff them with confetti and close up the hole with a homemade paste and tissue paper as a Mexican tradition she shared with the neighborhood kids. The idea behind it is that you looked for the eggs the same as an Easter Egg hunt but then you could crack these ones on people's heads. Phillip would drink with the dads and Mom would make her famous tacos for the lady across the street and it was perfect for a while. After they divorced, they all kinda disappeared from our daily lives. And the only people we really associated with were family members.

All along we were very close to my Mom's family. There were always a bunch of kids – my cousins and us all together. Phillip would take us to my Ama's house every Sunday and leave us there for the whole day to visit.

Most of what I remember from the ages five to about 11 is that my mom was very close to her family. They spent a lot of time together. My mom and her sisters would sip their beers and make *tamales*. In the kitchen they would gather, they would be in their slips because it was so hot and it was, after all, an all day affair. Even Tio Jose knew how to *embarra* (spread) the *masa* (dough) on the corn husk.

We would go to Walbridge Park on Broadway Street or just visit each other's houses. There were so many kids between them that there was always somebody to play with. I grew up very close to all my cousins and was particularly close with Angie. Angie was raised by Ama and Papa García, her father, Benjamin Garcia Jr., my mom's brother, who was a career man in the Air Force and away most of the time.

She was called *la gordita*, Spanish for chubby, but also used as an endearing term much like they called me *la güera* because I was light skinned.

Angie had chickenpox as a small child and had pox marks around one side of her nose and up the side of her face between her eye and temple. I don't know why that was always so noticeable to me. She had naturally curly hair, almost jet black. She was so cute and very sweet. I considered her my best friend.

Mom and Tia Lupe were like moms to Angie and her brother Gregory. Gregory was very close to Ama and my mom hated having to leave Angie when she and Phillip married. We had been living with the family in the same house since I was born. So us visiting them on the weekend was a way for Mom to remain close to Angie.

Sometimes we would walk to Kroger and stop into the *Segunda* (second hand store) along the way. One time Mom bought Angie and me these ballerina outfits, complete with tutus, and we were so excited to get home and try them on.

We came out of the bathroom, all excited doing a little dance, and Papa sat there screaming at us to go take them off, and called us *descaradas* (shameless). He was totally disgusted that Mom had bought them. They had words and we never saw those outfits again.

Childhood friends

With Susan McClain at Rachel's communion, February 1969

With Julie Heckman at Rachel's 8th grade graduation from Walbridge Elementary School

García family homes on Oliver street Toledo Ohio, photo from November 2020

Prima Sophia Arriaga Sánchez with Tia Catalina
García Castillo, Segur Street, July 1965

My mom, Rosa, with her
mom Angelina Garcia,
Carey, Ohio, 1980

Growing Up

One day Mom, Scottie, and I were walking home from Tia Lupe's house on Western Avenue and Mom pointed to a man who was on what I now know to be a paving machine, they were working on the street, and she said to me, "that's your dad right there." It was the first time I'd ever heard anything about my dad. I somehow knew that Phillip wasn't my dad, since I had always called him Phillip, but this new dad thing was very strange to me. It didn't really make sense to me, and I don't think I even replied, I didn't even know what to say. Not only did I *not* reply, but I never even gave it any thought until years later.

When Mom and Phillip divorced we didn't go to Ama's house much because mom didn't drive and there was no one to take us. On the rare occasion when she did have money for a cab, we could go that way, but that didn't happen very often. Once when we did we were so excited that when we got there we jumped out the car to go running up to the house and Scottie tripped and fell and hit the corner of his brow on the curb. My mom was so upset. That fall required an emergency room visit for a couple of stitches.

We were pretty far away from all of the people she loved – her Mom, her siblings Angie and Gregory, and I knew she was sad.

She would talk to her sister Tia Catita for hours on the telephone. And Angie called her every night to say goodnight to her.

When Tio Pancho was rushed to the hospital after having had a heart attack at home, Tia Lupe came to get us to take us to the family home on Oliver Street so the family could all be together with Ama. The same happened when Tia Catita passed – they came to tell mom and to take us to Oliver Street for the family to be together.

Catita was quite a bit older than my Mom but they were very close. They would go out together when they could and sit and gossip on the phone in Spanish, at that time I understood what they were saying. My mom spoke to me in Spanish all the time and I learned the language, I'm very proud to say. Not many of the cousins know the language but Angie and Gregory did as well as they spent all their time being raised in my grandparents' home. They only spoke Spanish and we wanted to communicate with them.

Once Phillip and Mom divorced there were no male role models except for Papa and he was mean and very strict.

We were only allowed to play in the back yard and if he could see any boys came out from the neighborhood he would make Angie and I come into the house. We were also not allowed to look out the window. There was a big picture window in the front of the house and he sat directly beside it most days looking out onto the street as he watched the television. At that time there were many houses and duplexes on the block with lots of kids running around. And we weren't friends with any of them.

Ama and Papa lived in the downstairs of a brick duplex. It was a property that my Tio Benjamin bought for the family to live in. At one time he lived upstairs briefly while home on visits. He had also acquired the property next door, another duplex, and eventually Catita lived there with her kids Izzy, Mary, and Joey until the time of her passing.

Tio Benjamin was away in the Air Force and Tia Lupe moved into Tia Catita's house when she passed and the only other brother, Tio Jose, lived across town with his wife and their seven children. We didn't get to see them very often and to this day I don't know what he did for a living during that time.

Aside from Tia Catita and Tia Lupe, Mom only had two really good friends Janie Duran and Beatrice Sudek. They and their husbands would come and get mom on occasion to take her out. But they never brought her back, imagine that. Because she would get out there and not want to come home when it was time. I know because they would tell me. Beatrice would say to me, "how can she not want to come home, when she has kids at home?" She said to me, "I have kids at home and I have to go home to take care of them!" And then she would laugh this little soft raspy laughter of hers, though I could see in her face that she didn't approve.

As we got a little older and boys came into the picture, it wasn't so bad that Mom would go out and stay out because we started sneaking boys into the house. And when I say we, by this time I had a couple girlfriends from school and Angie was practically living with us and we girls attracted lots of boys. We had our boyfriends and we would trade them about every other week. We didn't do anything, it was all very innocent and we just called each other boyfriend and girlfriend. That was until things did get a little serious between me and a boy whose attention I got while on a visit to Ama's house. I was in the seventh grade and he was in the eighth grade and he lived a few houses down from Ama's house. We spotted each other from across the back yards. I can't remember how we were able to speak to each other initially but we made a plan to sneak out and meet on the sidewalk to talk.

After Ama and Papa went to sleep, with Angie's help, I snuck out of her bedroom window and went to meet Rick. I wasn't scared at all. Here it was 12 AM midnight and we're walking on the sidewalk over by St. Peter and Paul church the next block over like nothing.

His family was Mexican as well and he had just the slightest accent. He pronounced my name not Rachel but Racho. He was so sweet and he talked softly to me and he sang me a song in Spanish on that first night as we sat on lawn chairs in his backyard. He had this way of throwing his head slightly back when he laughed. Instantly I was head over heels falling for this guy. My first boyfriend, and boy was he cute. Jet black hair and green eyes he was also taller than me and very thin. When I smell that same musk cologne to this day it takes me back to being in the seventh grade and walking and holding hands with Rick. I can't help it. It's one of the most exciting and wonderful times of my childhood that I'll never forget. Even though it ended badly and he crushed me, I'd never wish for it not to have happened. He was my first true love, you know how that feels, all warm and soft and cozy and brings tears to my eyes when I think about it.

About the same time Mom had met a man while out one night, who she brought home. His name was Bill Davis and he worked for Conrail Railroad as a conductor. Coincidentally, he would ride the trains that ran behind our house. As he began to spend more time at our house, and eventually even moved in, he would let Mom know the approximate time his train would be going by and she'd stand at the back door waiting. When the caboose went by he would use a lantern to wave up and down to her, it was the coolest thing. He'd be gone for several days at a time on his route that took him to Elkhart, Indiana, and when he returned it meant more frequent trips to Ama's house and going out to eat at our favorite restaurant, which at the time was The Acapulco on Western Avenue.

Bill belonged to the Elks Club and he took Mom once to buy a real fancy long dress for a night of dinner and dancing. He was dressed in a suit. Sometimes they would just go out for an evening and Mom would come home alone – after they'd gotten into a fight and he left her. But he always came back, eventually. They would leave the house so happy and she definitely was at her happiest when she was with him. I was not privy to any of their arguments, they kept it to themselves, but I guess he was used to things being a certain way.

Once I brought home a classmate for lunch who happened to be a black girl. Bill Davis didn't care for that, Mom had told me that I wasn't allowed to bring her home again. I remember he got upset with me because I didn't want to eat whatever it was they had cooked and he jumped up abruptly after I pushed my chair out to get up. That caused quite a scene as I started to cry at the table. All of a sudden he thought he was my boss and I resented Mom for allowing that to happen.

One year at Christmas time he got us in the car, Mom, Scottie, Angie, and I, and drove us to look at Christmas lights on River Road, where the houses looked like mansions. I thought they had the most beautiful lights there were. Something about the way they glowed at night, and the way I felt when I was there, and seeing the way all those beautiful homes lit up, made me dream of one day living on River Road. It became a big dream come true for me some forty years later. At Christmas time that same year, Angie and I found a bag of presents in the closet. They were the footie pajamas like what little kids wear and we put them on and went running in the snow around the house. We thought it was the funniest thing! Well Mom and Bill found out about it and took them back. We didn't get anything for Christmas that year.

He even went as far as taking the whole family, which included myself, my brother Scott, Angie, and Greg to meet his family who lived in Fayette, Ohio, about an hour away from Toledo.

Bill had four children from a previous marriage – three daughters and a son – and one of the daughters was a year younger than me. We spent time together on camping trips and swimming in Harrison Lake and going up north to Grayling, Michigan. His adult kids came to Toledo for a weekend and painted the inside of our small house. It was a really fun time in our lives.

Some of the gang in front of my childhood home.
Rachel Clark pictured in short hair sitting next to Keith Smith

THE TEENAGE YEARS

I had two very good friends in junior high: Kara and Dena. Kara's mom kept a very close eye on her but Dena's mom not so much and we were able to spend a lot of time together on the days and nights that Mom would be off on a binge before Bill Davis and sometimes while she was with him (their relationship was rocky to say the least). Alcohol always seemed to put a damper on things and nobody showed any signs of quitting. And so you learn what you live. At the time it all seemed natural. I had no idea that my family was dysfunctional. With boys coming into the picture, Mom being gone became a good thing, and I didn't take it personally anymore. I could use the telephone whenever I wanted, I could sit and talk to the neighborhood boys on the porch, and I had a bicycle I could ride all the way down Spencer Street if I wanted to.

First Love

New Years Eve while in the eighth grade is when I actually drank alcohol for the first time. I was already smoking at this time and Dena somehow managed to get a bottle of Sangria wine for us. I was breaking up with my boyfriend Rick because he decided he liked another girl. The memories I had of him singing to me... the smell of musk oil on his neck... the night we went to The Acapulco with my mom who bought us dinner was an actual first date ever. I remember he bought my mom a statue of the Virgin of Guadalupe they had in a display case. It brought tears to my eyes. It was just the sweetest gesture. All firsts for me and then he tells me after just a few months really that he likes someone else.

That New Years Eve night all the gifts he'd ever bought me, and there were a few, went into a brown paper bag and Dena and I and that bottle of Sangria headed over to his house.

It was a 35 minute walk one way, almost two miles, in the freezing cold. We walked right up the house and set that bag on his front porch and turned around and walked right back home.

The next time I saw him was when Angie and I had received an invite through a phone call from his older sister who was married to Angie's Godfather at the time to come to their house for dinner.

I had told Rick a big fat lie, now this is months later and it was such a stupid thing to do I don't know why I did it but I told Rick that I was pregnant. Not by him certainly that goes without saying because we never had any sexual relations. He was concerned enough about me that he took that information and shared it with his sister and her husband.

I was completely embarrassed when we arrived to find him there and he told me that he had confided in them about my situation, so I had to come clean to him at that moment. I still can see his face today and how disappointed he was in me. He just shook his head and didn't even say a word.

When he told them that it was a made up story they never once made me feel bad or tell me how stupid it was, and believe me I knew I knew right then and there. They had genuine concern for me and they were prepared to help me in any way they could. Even just to tell my mom. It was very hard to face him after that. Once he got his driver's license he would make an occasional trip to see me. We would just sit in his car and talk for a few minutes.

He just wanted to see me. I feel as though we had a special connection, even if only for a short while, it was very special to me and I could not ever hate him. I mean really, we were just kids.

childhood home

Angie, Dena, and Rachel age 15

THE DEATH OF BILL DAVIS

I was laying in bed one morning. I should've already been at school, but I overslept. The radio was on and I heard there had been an accident involving two trains that were on the same track and had collided. Was I dreaming, I thought? But I got up and made my way to school. I wasn't there long and they called me to go to the office. I found out that it had not been a dream and that Bill Davis was one of those killed in that terrible train crash that morning.

I can't remember if I walked home that day or if someone picked me up. When I got home I saw that Mom was just beside herself in disbelief. Who would rally around her? By this time all her time and energy was spent with him. His family lived out of town and the only one who was with her besides us was a neighbor lady, Beverly, who took it upon herself to be there for my mom and drive her to Fayette.

It was a devastating time first the loss and then the denial of my mom by his family in Fayette, Ohio. Afterwards my mom learned that she could possibly be eligible for his pension if they were considered to be common law husband and wife. She produced pictures of them painting the house as well as family having to be put on the stand, including myself, telling the judge that he did live with us and any other questions they had for us. I was so nervous that Mom gave me part of a Valium and then I just laughed on the witness stand. She got so mad at me. It was

probably more like just stupidly grinning. I don't know exactly what I did, but I definitely remember she was mad.

It was a long-drawn-out process in the court system and his family brought in a woman who they claimed he lived with as well but in the end my mom won her case.

She was no longer the welfare and food stamps recipient and now collected a very nice amount of money from the Railroad Retirement pension fund for myself and my brother Scott until we each turned 18. She was very generous with her money, too. We went out to eat more and she bought us clothes and nice things for the house. She bought Tia Lupe a new refrigerator that she needed. And of course had more money for drinking and she did more of that.

Barry Manilow came out with the song *This One's For You* in 1976, and, after Bill died, I remember Mom singing that song and crying over his loss.

Mom was pretty depressed for a long time. There was nothing I or anyone else could do to help her. I was just a teenager, how could I help her?

For a while I hung out with Carrie, a friend I'd known since grade school, who knew the bouncer at a downtown nightclub. That's how our little circle was let into The Country Palace. We would drink and dance to country music and Mom never knew because I would tell her that I was spending the night with my friend Carrie and come home the next day. I actually had another friend whose name was also Carrie, who had gotten pregnant very young and got married and so I had a couple of places where I could sleep away from home. And then on the nights that Mom was gone, the party was at our house and things sometimes got really out of control.

Bill Davis and Rosa Garcia

Inside our bungalow, L-R Angie, Tia Lupe, friend Steve Ibarra and Rachel

Rosa Garcia, Bill Davis, and Scottie

THE BOYS

I cannot move forward without so much as a mention of the boys from my neighborhood. They were the greatest bunch to go to school with and I cannot imagine not having had them in my life. My grade school years were the best school years of my life even with all that was going on at home. I don't claim to have had a bad childhood, the Lord knows it could've been way worse. My friends were such a saving grace for me I realized so many years later when I looked back and thoughts of them came flooding back.

But the boys were special too.

Howard was the same age as me. He lived down the block and he's one who was always involved in a contest to see if I would like him. He would walk me to school. And he'd sit on the front porch listening for hours while Mom told us ghost stories – he'd be all scared. He had blond hair and beautiful blue eyes and surely a great catch later, too, as he matured he got a perm and looked just like Peter Frampton. In high school he played the trumpet and you could hear him a block away practicing in his house.

Tom had the biggest crush on Angie. He would come and sit outside on the side porch and they would talk through the window. It was all that Mom would allow. He shot himself after high school.

Keith was my boyfriend for a little while. We would meet down the block and I would ride him on the handlebars of my bike and we would just hang out down the street. He lived farther away than I was allowed to go, but his Grandma lived just down the street and if he spent the night at her house he would wait for me in the freezing cold so we could walk together to school. He was the cutest, I have to admit, out of all the boys. He had dark brown hair and wore swoop bangs. His hair was straight. He had a shy way about him and when he laughed he always put his head down. Sadly he shot himself as well after he'd married and had a couple kids. At the time he was working as an electrician in one of the newer hospitals that was being built in the area.

David was sweet and I really liked him, he had a nasally sounding voice and it was hard getting past that but we liked each other for a while.

Larry was the smallest of the bunch and he had lots of freckles and his voice was raspy. He had dark hair and it swooped down covering one eye and he would always be jerking his head to get the hair out of his eyes.

Brian lived the farthest away but he would babysit for his sister and she lived just down the street. They rode their bikes in groups of four or five right down the middle of the street. We could see them coming and the excitement would build. We'd just stand out there on the street talking about nothing.

Before letting us go outside, Mom would always tell us *pórtate trista* - meaning that we should carry ourselves "sad." We were not allowed to laugh with or carry on with them. At the end of our street there was a road that led down to the creek and they liked to ride down there and throw stones or rocks into the creek. I mean they were eighth grade boys. Perfectly harmless.

During this time my old friends Julie and Sue were no longer hanging out with me. After the eighth grade graduation they went on to high school and I didn't really see them again even though we lived right across the street from each other. I don't know if their parents told them they couldn't. We never talked about it but there were a lot of kids coming in and out of our house. When Mom was out we had a houseful. And if she came home we would sneak them out the back door as she was coming in the front. Hey, I didn't say it was right but this was my life. I had no real role models to teach me any differently.

Mom was busy with her friends and going out and meeting different men after Bill died. Angie and I were just running a muck. Not going to school, not going to work like I was supposed to.

One night Mom came home and had some beer and burritos she brought us to eat. I was already sleeping and Angie and then boyfriend Randy were still awake and she invited Randy to have a beer with her and so he did.

She came into the room where I was sleeping and told me to get up and she had burritos. I told her no I'm not getting up, it was like 3 AM. She got mad at me and threw the burrito at my back! Angie came for her and took her back out to the dining room and told her that they would eat the burrito with her and just to leave me alone since I was tired. She mumbled something about me not being appreciative, that damn burrito was all over my back and the bed and it was so hot it burned through my top.

When The Drinking Starts

Somebody got their hands on some moonshine. By this time the circle had changed a little bit. Angie and I were introduced to some of Dena's friends from the other side of the Anthony Wayne Trail. They were a little older. On this particular day Mom wasn't home and we were skipping school and had this moonshine. I don't remember much of that day other than the fact that Mom was not expected to be home, I believe she was on a binge.

At the time of this writing I Googled, "is it rape if you're drunk?" All I can say is I was so drunk I couldn't even talk and it was over so fast I was left dazed and confused like what the F just happened? This guy was not my boyfriend. He took me by the hand and led me into my mom's room. He pulled my pants down and had his way with me and I was unable to even speak. I guarantee you if he'd been in my situation that act would've never happened. I've thought about it over the years and it was such a violation on me. This guy was not a part of our circle on any other given day not before or after, what was he even doing there I guess I'll never know.

How many women have gone through this very thing and carry the shame that goes with it? All these years, I felt as though I was as much to blame because I allowed myself to be in a situation to be taken advantage of. And that way of thinking is so wrong.

Nobody has the right to help themselves to another person's body, ever!

When the day comes, and it most definitely will, eventually, like it came for me, and I found my courage and was able to talk about it and say your name you were outed! It's no longer a secret, and you didn't get away with anything.

You may think that nobody knows, but the all important God knows all for He is Omnipresent.

It's unfortunate but unless people can choose to do evil, nobody gets the promise of a pain free life.

L-R Rachel and friend Carrie with John and baby Colleen

Hard to believe but less than a year after this picture was taken, I would be pregnant. I was so young, just 16 years old.

Teen Pregnancy

When I first laid eyes on Lee he was flipping burgers at McDonald's on Broadway. I knew he was a brother to one of my classmates and that he was four years older. Shortly after that, I heard that he had joined the army.

This night, though, he was home on leave and when I went to my friend Carrie's house he was there, and he had bought beer and wine which we drank and one thing led to another. Because you see this is what alcohol was doing to me personally. It allowed me the freedom to feel older than my 16 years of age and therefore do grown up things. I had no inhibitions. I didn't even say no, I just went along with having sex with him.

I had broken up with a boyfriend a couple of months earlier, one who I was frequently with at the Downtown Nightclub and so when I missed my period I knew who the father was. But what I didn't know was that he was engaged to be married to a German woman at the same time that he was home on leave getting drunk and having sex with me.

Neither of us practicing safe sex, I got pregnant on a one night stand (that's what they were called). Here I was, pregnant for real now. I couldn't even be the one to tell my mom, because someone else did. I never asked who.

I didn't see Lee again that year. He had left to go back to Germany, narrowly escaping the blizzard we had here in Toledo – the Blizzard of 1978. We were all together at Ama's house and

Tia Lupe lived next door. We were able to keep up with what was happening with the world outside through a small radio in the kitchen. We listened for hours as phone call after phone call came in, someone reaching out for help for a family member to inquire if they were safe. No traffic was able to move and if you had a snowmobile you would be asked to help the community move groceries or transport doctors and nurses to work.

It paralyzed the city. It was referred to as The Storm of the Century, as it killed 50 people in Ohio and caused at least a 100 million dollars in damage. We got 13 inches of snow, wind gusts that topped 50 miles an hour, and sub zero wind chill temperatures.

Angie had a baby and she was only about four months old when this happened. They sent Gregory and me to the store to buy some formula and it was quite a trek. The wind was blowing the snow, not to mention it was waist high in some areas. I didn't think I was going to make it when Gregory told me to just wait there for him. Oh hell no you'll never find me, I thought and just pushed forward.

Once we got to the main road we could see people walking in the street pulling sleds of whatever few groceries they could get from Kroger on Broadway. It was quite a sight, nothing but white blinding snow as far as the eye could see.

February came and with no period in sight and my slight frame at only 98 pounds, it didn't take long for me to start showing. I informed Lee through a letter and he'd already gotten married in Germany. My friend Carrie was the one to tell me. I had no intentions nor did I want to be with him but I would've liked for him to take responsibility for the baby I was carrying. That would not happen as I heard from him claiming that he could not have kids. And until the baby actually arrived there really wasn't anything anybody could do.

Mom informed the Friesners (Robert's parents), who had been sending Christmas presents for me, of my pregnancy and they threw me a baby shower. It was the first time I'd met them along with Robert Friesner. I still wasn't sure if he was my dad but he was there and seemed very happy to meet me. Mom and I went and it was like I'd known these people all my life. The shower was great, the food, cake, and gifts. They went all out. I was very appreciative and Grandma Friesner could not have been any kinder.

When the time came for me to deliver my baby girl I was totally unsuspecting of what was to happen. I went into labor running in the rain from Ama's house to Tia Lupe's house, which was right next door. I was running because it was pouring rain. This was October 5 and she was born on October 6, at 3:23 AM. It was the toughest thing I'd ever done! Oh gosh the pain I remember it well, but when it was all done I had this beautiful little human who belonged to only me and I just cried happy tears. I vowed that it would be just her and me and that she didn't need her dad when she had me. He'd denied her and it hurt so bad. Made me wonder, really, really wonder, for the first time what was the real story with my own dad. Why were the Friesners told that I was their grandchild and who was this man my mom had pointed out to me on the street that day when I was just 11 years old?

As soon as I could, I went to apply for assistance in the form of a monthly check and food stamps for baby formula and I was given a small amount because I lived at home with my mom though she was not responsible for the baby. So I took this beautiful little baby home who I named Rose, I just cherished taking care of her. Everything came instinctively. I just loved her so much I would hold her and cry. I loved her so much.

I had no plans for the future. I had no way of knowing how I was going to care for her, I wish I could say I had.

Shortly after baby Rose was born, Mom sold the house I'd lived in for 13 years, whre I grew up, and moved us out of the neighborhood. It was time to go for sure. The neighbors didn't like us for being so rowdy all the time. The police had been called to our house several times and the neighbor directly across once gave me the middle finger standing right in front of her picture window. I don't recall how old I was at the time and I didn't even know what it meant but there she was waving it at me with this great big smile on her face.

It was the place I'd caught a glimpse of Mom having sex in the car parked in the driveway. I fell asleep on the sofa waiting for her and I awoke to the sound of a car running outside. The driveway was right next to the house and as I adjusted my sleepy eyes to see what I could see I saw a man's butt moving up and down in the back seat. I quickly moved from the window, having a sense that I wasn't supposed to see that. And I just lay there waiting for her to come in the door some time later.

Sometimes she would bring them in and other times not.

By this time I no longer had any friends on the block or off the block. So much had happened there, like playing spades at the kitchen table all hours of the night. Or when we had Dena hidden in our attic with her baby brother Scottie because they were going to have to go to a home. Dena's mom liked to be in the bar as well and there were times when they didn't have food or electricity or diapers for her little brother Scottie. Dena was going to the children's home if we hadn't helped her. So that's what we were trying to do when Mom heard a noise and walked into our room and saw her up in the attic. Dena did go to a home – we all felt so bad for her and her little brothers she had two of them, Jimmy and Scottie. Mom tried to help by telling them that she could stay with us, but our home wasn't so stable either.

At one time we had a dryer full of beer cans. It didn't work anyway. Most times we had to dry our clothes in the oven. I had a pair of pants that had grill burn marks on them from too many times forgetting they were in there.

Rachel, age 17, and Rose

Moving to a New House

Moving to a new house was great! It was a two story, three bedroom home. A very beautiful home that one of my classmates had lived in and one that I never would have pictured us living in.

It had an open living room and dining room with big windows to let sunshine in. I especially liked the dining window that had a built-in settee, although that window overlooked the body shop right next door, I took much care ensuring that it was always sparkling clean. And the front porch ran the entire length of the house. I can't tell you how many nights were spent out there just sitting and watching the traffic go by until all hours of the night. It was our favorite pastime during the summertime.

By this time I'd turned 18 and being new in the neighborhood, I quickly found the neighborhood tavern two blocks away that became my little place to hang out, if I wasn't dancing at the nightclub Renee's.

I would put baby Rose to sleep and go down to Bogarts for a couple of beers and an occasional after party. Romantically, there was no one currently in my life and I liked it that way. By this time I had a real distaste for men. Why? Because the men in my life up to this point sucked as role models.

There were no men to look up to to help the women. Not in my life. My stepdad Phillip tried to be – he was the only grandpa Rose knew. He paid his child support and saw Scott when he could and as Scott got older they spent even more time together and he took us once to see the movie *Saturday Night Fever* and to a car show.

It was only the second time I'd been to a theatre. The first was when I was 13 and Mom took Scott and me to the Pantheon in downtown Toledo and tried to pass me off as being 12. But I spoke up and proclaimed that I was actually 13. She was so mad at me at having to pay full price for my admission, she never took us again.

My stepdad Phillip was an only child and when his dad died he was a devoted son handling things for his mom until she passed from Alzheimer's. They would have lunch out everyday, and he would also take her for all her hair appointments. Alzheimer's is a terrible, sad disease. I hated seeing her like that.

But he too would take advantage of some of the younger girls from his neighborhood, after he and mom divorced, and by that I mean teenage girls. Underage girls definitely. I can recall one instance when we were going to use his home for a baby shower for Angie.

We arrived early to get things set up and one of these girls came out of his room walking shyly past us and out the back door never saying a word. I just looked at him and he looked back at me biting on his lower lip with eyebrows lifted high. He knew he'd been busted. But that didn't mean anything to him I'm sure.

On occasion I would go to the dance club with Dena and a group of girls from her side of the trail. Through Dena I met Amy McNeil. She turned out to be quite a fighter. She'd get a few drinks in and don't look at her wrong because she'd come after you. We would meet up with a group of guys from the university area, they were all students from Saudi Arabia, and we just danced with them.

Yeah, there were a couple of hook ups, but mostly just someone to drink with and dance with and then maybe go out to eat breakfast afterwards. They had money and they always paid, their parents would send them money every month on top of paying for all their expenses while they were in school.

I'd gotten my license right at 16. Mom sent me to driving school so that we could have a car and we wouldn't have to take cabs anymore. So I was always the one driving. Sometimes I don't even remember how I got home. By God's grace, that's how. I'd wake up in my bed and not remember getting in it. Not bragging, just trying to be honest. Trying to accept and take responsibility for the things I know I did wrong.

One night I do remember coming in and the front door was open, not the screen just the inside door. It was like 4 AM. I walked in and went straight to the kitchen where the lights were on and there was Mom asleep at the table with Rose asleep in her high chair right beside her. It hurt me so bad. I got my baby and closed up the house and took her upstairs to bed. I left Mom sleeping at the table.

Mom had a new boyfriend and his name was Doug. He was also a railroad worker but had been in a motorcycle accident, walked with a limp, and was on disability as he was no longer able to work. He moved in with her and was very nice to all of us.

It was during this time that Mom gave up alcohol. She quit cold turkey. One day she said to me that she wasn't going to drink anymore. She said she wanted to save her money so she could take a trip to Germany.

Angie was now living there because her husband Randy had joined the Army and was stationed in Germany. Angie was going to be giving birth to their third child and wanted Mom to come and stay and help her for a little while.

I never thought I'd see the day that my mom would be getting on a plane. She had to fly out of Detroit, it was Doug and myself and Tia Lupe, Scott, and Rose who went to Detroit Airport that day. I was so scared for her and I knew that she was too, but nonetheless she got on that plane. I'd never seen her so determined to do something, I thought it was so brave of her and I was very proud of her at that moment.

I finally found out my biological father had denied me.

As the story goes, Mom had separated from the man I'm named after, Robert Friesner, and, while singing in a piano bar, she met and then had an affair with Jim Cappelletty. Unbeknownst to her, Cappelletty was married and had a family. When Mom told him she was pregnant, he told her that he was married with children and denied that I could possibly be his. Mom was the daughter of migrant workers; she was 24 years old and she didn't have any money to hire a lawyer. That's when I believe she told Robert Friesner that I was his. But there was always that question... she never had a test done to establish paternity.

My mom carried me alone, no husband to support her, and when she was released from Mercy Hospital after delivering me, it was Tio Pancho who picked the two of us up and brought us home to Ama and Papa's house on Oliver Street. She cared for me like I'd cared for my own daughter – with the help of family members, because the men didn't own up to the responsibility. Honestly, I didn't want Lee in my life. I didn't know him, and I didn't even want to get to know him. It didn't even bother me when I found out that he'd brought home his German wife and they were living at his parents' home until they found a place of their own.

I'd not had a job to speak of other than a short stint in a restaurant that Tio Benny had opened up, even though they didn't pay me. It was a joke, the whole business was a joke. Half the time we didn't have what was on the menu, other times someone would burn the beans and you could smell them throughout the entire restaurant. So my getting paid was also a joke because Tia Lupe would take the money from the cash register and proceed to her office next door which happened to be George's bar. But it gave me a little taste of what it was like to go to a job for the first time. Mom would give me a little money and I had a welfare check, a small one coming in each month for diapers and baby formula, and the occasional enchilada dinner at The Acapulco.

Rose was two years old when I found out that Lee was looking for me. He'd wanted to be in our lives, to be a father, and to be with me. He told my mom first, I don't know how or where. I didn't bother to ask, but she came and was the one to tell me. She told me that he deserved to be given the chance since he was Rose's father. No way... I wanted nothing to do with it. I hid from him for days. I knew he was coming to the bar looking for me. One night I caught sight of him sitting at the bar and I made a quick exit out the back door with friends to go to the Speedway where there was a concert going on. But since Mom was all for it, I couldn't hide myself for very long.

One of the first times we went out together was to his brother's house and his wife Carrie, friends of mine before I met Lee. They had bought a house and were living across town.

Lee picked Rose and I up, it was the first time he was seeing his daughter aside from once when she was still an infant. It was my birthday and with Carrie's help he'd bought me a gift of a couple pairs of jeans and a top. It was all very pleasant and we'd hit it off right away and before I knew it Mom had allowed him to move into the house with us. I was really taken aback by this – that she would allow this to happen – but I went with it because he was renting a room in the same neighborhood. He had a job and started taking care of us and it wasn't long before we moved out into our own little house in the old south end of Toledo that he rented.

It was a very small house that reminded me of the house on Pere Street where I had grown up. It was a bungalow – two bedrooms, living room, dining room, and small kitchen in the back of the house and a second bedroom was in back of that. It was a kind of strange layout, with the second bedroom in the very front of the house, off the dining room. Back then you rented month to month, you didn't have to sign a lease, which was good, since we weren't there very long as I found out that I was expecting again soon after we settled.

In the bungalow we'd made a nice little place. Mom had given me two beautiful red velvet chairs. I just loved them so much and I didn't ask her for them. They were in the house that she bought and she just asked me as I was getting ready to move if I'd wanted to take them with me. I was thrilled! Our couch, also given to us, sat on three legs and the fourth was a brick. We were also given a dining room table that we spent hours on sanding and refinishing.

One morning we'd gotten up and got ready to leave the house and when we went out to get in the car the car was gone! Oh gosh, it'd been stolen, so we thought, but came to find out it was repossessed. Apparently we weren't doing so good after all.

There was no partying at this time, we were just struggling to pay our bills. I'm not sure what the money situation was at that time. I wasn't privy to that information, I knew that Lee was going through a divorce and that his German wife had gone back to Germany. I didn't ask any question about his financial situation, it's just not something I thought of at the time. So it turned out we needed to go back to my mom's house for another short while until we figured things out.

I don't know why I never asked him what happened. I heard later from my friend Carrie that there was infidelity going on on both sides but I have no way of knowing because I never asked and I didn't care. I wish I'd asked now. Ever hear that expression, when someone shows you who they are, believe them!

Once I visited my friend Carrie, while she and her husband Roger, Lee's brother, were renting a small house behind Lee's parents house. Lee had just got home from the Army with his German wife, and my friend Carrie took Rose out to the main house where Lee's parents lived so they could see the baby. They knew that baby Rose was my baby and that I was claiming that Lee was the father.

Years later I found out that a comment had been made about baby Rose looking like Lee. Because she did and I don't know how anyone could deny a precious little baby.

Lee got a job as a manager for Taco Bell as I continued along in my second pregnancy.

One night we were all asleep upstairs when Angie, now back from Germany, came into the room to wake us up. She said that something was going on outside with our car. So we jumped up and ran to my mom's bedroom as it faced the street and out the window we could see that our car was being toilet papered by a couple of drunk women.

They were falling all over each other laughing with the paper in hand and I'm yelling at Lee. Does he know what the hell is going on? He is swearing that he doesn't and I'm threatening to call the police. They finished their little song and dance while we continued to watch and I was livid. I just knew there was something he wasn't telling me.

The next day he went to work and confronted the two coworkers of his and according to him they were very drunk and very remorseful for what they did.

I guess I really didn't want them to lose their jobs. I just wished they hadn't done such a thing. I was pregnant. I'd wished they'd had more respect for their manager and his wife. But I blew it off, too. It was kinda funny. And they'd left four beers behind, still bound from a six pack, laying on the grass right beside the curb.

My beautiful second baby girl Ann came in August of the following year and we married in October.

Lee and I were married in downtown Toledo outside the Lucas County courthouse by the justice of the peace. Angie was there with her kids Colleen and Randy and baby Selina. My own Rose had just turned three and Ann was just two months old. Mom and Doug were there, too. Afterwards we all went to George's to have a few drinks and celebrate. We shared a few laughs about how the little kids were running up and down the stairs of the Court House and you could hear a fire engine blaring its horns as it came down the street. And then back to Mom's house with all the kids.

Marriage

We bought our first home together as a married couple using the VA loan. It was a two story that sat right beside an alley. Painted the color yellow with brown trim, it was one of the more attractive houses in the neighborhood and stood out on the block. An old man lived alone in it and we knew him from the nightclub George's. It was up by Broadway close to Jones Junior High School, a very nice area at the time. One block away from Kroger, and taverns like Georges's and Sotteks and Gino's Pizza. It was a big home, it had three bedrooms, living room, dining room, and foyer – all with natural dark wood work throughout and big double paned windows for lots of sunlight.

It was a comfortable location and a beautiful home, but as soon as we moved in, things started going downhill.

Rose was three and Ann was eight months. I took a part time job working at Frisch's Big Boy restaurant downtown also known as the Hi Level. The Hi Level Bridge, painted blue, connected the Old South End to East Toledo. I had to take the bus on most occasions to get there, but I didn't mind. I always liked riding the bus. Working at Frisch's was my first real job. I was making $2.01 an hour plus tips. And we'd found this tavern that we had begun frequenting. I think Lee's younger brother Danny was the one who told us about it. It wasn't near our home, so we'd only gone there a few times. When one night things got really bad, really fast. Lee was drinking tequila and we hadn't been there but a couple hours and we got into a disagreement over something and he went nuts!!!

We left the tavern and I refused to get into the car with him and I just started walking down Western Avenue. He called me over to the car where he was driving really slow on the pretense of wanting to tell me something, I must've gotten really close to his car door, the next thing I knew he'd grabbed a hold of my arm and stepped on the gas causing me to have to run beside his car! Only when he heard someone yelling from their front porch did he let go. A guy in another car apparently saw what was happening also and asked if I wanted some help and Lee threatened to kick his ass if he didn't mind his own business, so I just got into the car. It might sound crazy – and I would tell my children otherwise to yell or scream for help – but I just didn't think of screaming at the time. Maybe it was because I was miles from home and I just wanted to get home. Or maybe it was because I worried someone might get hurt who'd try to come to my aid. Lee was acting out of character even for him. He'd already threatened physical harm and its 3 AM.

Tia Lupe had been staying with us and she had just bought a handful of cast iron pans that someone was selling at George's and she'd shown me them earlier in the day. Lee and I argued the whole way. I ended up getting in the car for the drive home, and we continued to argue all the way. When we were almost home Lee said something about taking the kids, I told him he was drunk and he wasn't going to take the kids anywhere.

When we walked in the front door I stood on the steps leading to the second floor where the bedrooms were, trying to block him from going up. I told him he was not going to take the kids. That's when he grabbed me around my throat and with just one arm he threw me up the stairs. Tia Lupe started yelling at him and with all of us yelling, it wasn't long before I could hear the kids crying in their bedroom. Lee got hold of the cast iron pans and started throwing them at the windows one by one. He'd broken six windows, three double panes. I can't tell you who called the police. I don't know if it was Tia Lupe or my elderly neighbor after hearing commotion, but we heard sirens and then they, the police, were at the front door.

I directed them upstairs where he'd gone into the bathroom and they found that he'd jumped out of a window. They searched for him on foot and found him a few doors down hiding under someone's porch. They forced him out and arrested him. I'd never experienced anything so violent in my life. We were so shaken up. Lee blamed it all on the tequila.

The next day I had to have the windows boarded up and he was released on his own recognizance though had to appear in court at a later time. I allowed him to come right back into the house.

Tia Lupe left and she wanted nothing to do with him. I could not leave my home, it just wasn't an option I thought I had, and nobody told me any different.

Another time I'd made a big mistake by telling Lee about an old boyfriend. I don't know if I mentioned it while we were drinking. But I had liked this guy way before Lee was even in the picture. Truth is he'd gotten into trouble with the law a few times and had been locked away most of the time, and was locked away all during my pregnancy. But by the time Lee and I got together he was actually out of jail and in Vegas with some big time drug dealers. So it was a blessing in disguise that we didn't stay together. I don't know that I could've made any difference in his life, but I didn't know that at the time. So every chance that Lee got he would throw him up in my face.

He would insinuate that maybe Donnie could do things better, or maybe if Donnie were there I'd be happier. Lee liked to make remarks about Donnie often because he knew that I was happy with him and at one time I wanted to be with him. I could not get him to see that things were different now that the times had changed and that I no longer wanted to be with Donnie but for some reason he still felt threatened by him.

We had back then what we called girls night out and I ran into Donnie Winter at Ladies Choice bar. It was the first time we'd seen each other since I'd gotten married. It was all very innocent. I ran out of gas that night trying to get home and arrived back at the house very late. I called my brother-in-law Danny, Lee's brother and the husband of my sister-in-law, who was with me that night, to bring me gas and he did. I had just left their house after dropping her off.

When I entered the house Lee was waiting for me and was very mad. He cornered me against the washing machine and kept asking me where I'd been, I told him about having run out of gas and calling Danny for help. He wasn't satisfied with my answer and kept repeating it over and over and every time he would ask he would punch me in the arm, punching a little harder each time. This went on until I pushed my way past him and threatened to call the police on him if he didn't stop. This resulted in him ripping the phone out of the wall and eventually going to bed sneering at me as he walked away, and I went to sleep on the sofa.

The next morning when I woke up he was already gone on a hauling job with his brothers and dad who owned a hauling business.

I didn't expect the kids would still be sleeping and all was quiet as I walked up the stairs first entering the baby's room. Ann was eight months old and she slept in a room I'd painted bright yellow for her, the crib sat along the left wall as you entered the room and upon entering I got this whiff of something in the air, a sweet smell of a urinated diaper was what it was. I looked down into her crib and she was laying on her back looking up at me strangely. Her cheeks were red, I mean really red. I began to freak out, wondering what was wrong with my baby as she just lay there motionless. I reached down to pick her up and she was hot. Her whole little body under the sleeper felt like it had just come out of the dryer and when I lifted her up her eyes started to roll back into her head. I started screaming, "Oh my God," and I ran to the phone, forgetting that it had been disabled. By this time Rose had heard me and she was crying not knowing what was happening.

A neighbor, an elderly lady named Dolly, called for emergency help for us and the first to show up was the fire department. They wrapped Ann in soaking wet bath towels and when an ambulance arrived we all went to the hospital.

Ann had an ear infection and it caused the high fever and thus caused the convulsions. There was a misunderstanding between Lee and myself about whether or not I was going to allow them to do a spinal tap at the hospital, to which I say never would I have allowed it. They wanted to and asked me and I said no.

When Lee finally arrived at the hospital I'd been through the worst day of my life. Not only going through that with my baby Ann, I looked like I'd been beat up. I was completely bruised down my arm from the night before where he had been punching me and I never even considered what I looked like – must've been one hot mess. I just wanted him to take us home and I wanted everything to be better. All was forgotten and forgiven, that is until the next time.

I was totally committed to my marriage, I worked for literally nickels and dimes as a waitress. I took care of my two girls and learned to cook, somewhat, to keep house. We didn't want for anything. We had nice clothes, nice furniture, and we had family around us. We would go out on occasion. There was a group of friends from Frisch's and we would meet after work at Frank's Inn.

Lee's brother Danny turned us on to the neighborhood tavern – the place where Lee had too many shots of Tequila and then busted out all those windows at home. The truth is I loved Lee. He was a good provider and a good father, but he was also a big flirt who loved flirting with all my friends. He was definitely the life of the party. Telling jokes and making people laugh most times just leaving me shaking my head, especially after telling Mexican jokes! In private my friends would tell me how Lee would flirt with them and ask them out. I never believed it. I always took it as he was just joking around. And they would tell me that they didn't think he was joking. Lee and I would argue because I would confront him on it and he would say they were just lying. How could it be that all my friends are just lying? I didn't see the reason behind that, I told him. And so I started watching him a little closer and he knew it. But of course I remained blind because we see what we want to see, or don't want to see, and the alcohol blurs your vision as well, and little by little I started to care less and less.

Living in our new home was short lived when one day our sofa leg went clean through the floor. We pulled back the carpeting and discovered that the previous owner had laid a cheap particle board in an effort to hide termite damage and we decided we would let the house go back to the bank. It was a terrible decision, but we felt we had no choice and would have to file for bankruptcy at a later time because of it. We'd been deceived.

Once again we were on the move. This time renting a downstairs duplex from Lee's sister Molly and her husband Tom, where our son and third child would be born.

It was in the same neighborhood as the first house that we rented just a few doors down. A really nice area with kids of all ages for the girls to play with, though they preferred the neighbors next door – a Mexican family – Gloria and Gus Arredondo (the kids called him Gas - lol) with three girls and two boys, one girl Joyce was a foster child.

Lee got a little braver and I continued to turn a blind eye and the alcohol didn't help my case at all. He started denying certain behaviors, telling me that I was drunk and didn't know what I was talking about and yes that was true a lot of the time. It didn't take much after working. We'd hit the bar around 10 or 11 PM and it was so convenient to have a babysitter who lived right next door. Joyce was 14 and so sweet and loved the kids and I paid her a dollar an hour. Most evenings the kids would be up only a short while and then she would put them to bed. And we could come in at 2:30 AM or later if we went out for breakfast, which we sometimes would do. There was usually a group of us and we would go to Frisch's because it was open 24 hours a day, never mind that we'd just left there.

Lee's younger brother Roger, who had been married to my friend Carrie, found himself divorced and single, raising his two children alone. I introduced him to one of the girls I worked with and they hit it off and soon after married. They rented a house right across the street from us. Now Roger was not a drinker and Marsha was, so there were problems from the get go. He had his two kids and Marsha had a small daughter herself, Jennifer. Their marriage lasted about three years before they parted ways due to her drinking.

Marsha would be the first of my friends to pass from complications from the abuse of alcohol, she was 45 years old. I met her when we were 24 years old.

Marsha Loboschefski 1963-2007

A Son Is Born

On February 26, 1984, my little boy came into the world. Lee and I were so happy with the arrival of our beautiful and healthy baby boy. I don't know about now, but back then they kept mother and baby in the hospital for three days to recuperate and bond. I loved getting visitors, some brought me flowers even. I remember a planter that was shaped like a pair of booties with a blue ribbon and it contained an assortment of plants. I thought it was so thoughtful and when I took my baby boy home I was so proud of what we'd made together and of our little family.

Lee was so excited to go to Frank's Inn about three days after I'd gotten out of the hospital as he wanted to pass out some cigars he'd bought earlier in the day to his friends. I was happy for him to go and share the news with his friends and sister Molly was going with him, I was still recovering from having given birth and was happy to remain at home.

I was naturally a night owl and of course with a new baby sleep was not going to come early this evening. At about 2 AM the anticipation started for Lee to return home. I wanted to hear about his night and what his friends had to say about the new baby being home. Frank, the owner, was sure to be excited and happy for us and I pictured him laughing behind the bar and giving Lee a celebratory drink on the house.

2:30 AM came and nothing. It was 3 AM when I heard the door open to the duplex and footsteps leading up the stairs to

Molly's apartment, the door opened and closed and I waited a few minutes longer, sure that Lee would be next to come in the door but it was silent. No one was coming. I waited a few more minutes and then I picked up the phone to call upstairs to Molly. When she answered I asked her where Lee was. I told her that I'd heard her come in. She reassured me that he was coming behind her that she'd gotten a ride home from someone else. So I thought, okay he must've been held up in the parking lot maybe talking with his brother Danny or anyone else from the bar. Never would I ever have imagined what he was actually doing in that parking lot that night.

He finally came in about 4:30 AM and I was hot! I'd been pacing the floors. I wasn't worried that something had happened to him, no it was much worse than that! He walked in with his head down, unable to even look at me! Immediately I demanded to know where he'd been and he couldn't even respond, couldn't lie his way out of it, didn't even try. He tried to go to bed and not even respond to my anger threats of beating the hell out of him. He turned off the lights and I turned them back on. He started to laugh which just made me all the more mad. Then he started to get mad at me because I guess I was just annoying him.

Let me just say that nothing good was taking place in Frank's Inns parking lot after hours.

That night I became a different person. I'd left the house briefly. I went to the only place I could go at 6 AM and that was to Frisch's. I ordered a cup of coffee and just sat there not knowing what to do. What could I do? I had a five day old baby at home and two other kids. I had no choice but to go back home.

How could I tell anyone what had happened? How could I face anyone? Most of all it hurt so bad I just wanted the pain to go away and I wanted him to take the pain away. What I remember next about that is sitting in the dining room. He was sitting on a dining chair and I was on his lap and I was sobbing and he was telling me how sorry he was that it didn't mean anything and there beside us is our little baby fast asleep in his crib. He didn't have a room of his own; his crib was right there in the dining room. I have never told this story before. Only four of us knew what happened before now. I'd never met this woman before and never heard her name until that night. She was married and her husband was well known to others and I wanted so badly to go to him and tell him, but I couldn't bring myself to do it. Because it happened to me and put my marriage in turmoil I couldn't do that for someone else, I just couldn't.

When I think about this and how I felt having been so betrayed and still wanting him to hold me and take away the pain that he caused, it makes me wonder. Why? But today I know the answer to that and it's because I had no one else to call to take that pain away from me. Not my mom, not my dad, all I had and knew was him. My whole life was him and my kids and I guess he could've done almost anything to me and I'd still be right there with him.

We have choices as women, isn't that what we want? What do we do with our bodies and our reproductive system? So why then aren't we as vocal when it comes to the men in our lives and what we will tolerate from them, especially where there are children involved?

Had I left him very early on I wouldn't have had the kids I have today and I can't imagine what my life would be like without them, today my life would've been very different.

I've always been a firm believer that everything happens for a reason and I may not have all of the answers this side of Heaven but I do believe that one day all of my questions will be answered. It's not my nature to question God and ask him, "Why me?" It has become my nature to trust in Him and let things be as they may and know that He works out everything for my good. He has never let me down when no one was there for me.

Ann age 3, Rose age 7

Junior, 10 months

Lesson 1
Don't Let Anger Rule

It was something my friend and co-worker Chris Villegas Romo said while we were having lunch one day that made the mama claws come out, and instantly made me angry!

She was further along on the tough love where her kids were concerned than I was and when she said that I ought to be doing some things differently, I reacted in the only way in which I knew how, because in my mind I was being criticized.

How dare she talk to me that way. Was it her tone? Was it something I didn't agree with or hadn't thought of myself, and does it really matter at this point?

She proceeded to then do something that would change the course of my entire life.

She apologized to me. She apologized to me for hurting my feelings!

Never had it occurred to me that I'd had my feelings hurt, feelings were never spoken about while I was a child and growing up.

As I look back now I see that anger took the place of many things.

Of being scared, of feeling lonely and unloved. It took the place of needs not being met, of being left, left out, and left behind. Anger took the place of betrayal and resentment. Physical and verbal attacks. Anger took the place of being hungry, today it's called "hangry" - imagine that. Any other emotions that could have possibly come because I was without emotion but full of anger.

As told by my mom, when I was three years old, Papa asked me to hand him an ashtray from the table, and I refused. He asked me again and added, "por favor, Mija," (please, darling) and still I refused. Mom said she took me by the hand trying to force me to pick up the ashtray all the while still refusing, and, no, I never did give him the ashtray.

It makes me wonder if that stubbornness shown at such a young age wasn't in preparation for the life that was ahead.

I WISH I KNEW THEN...

Many women go through stuff like this, and way worse, and feel like they don't have any choices. But in hindsight if I'd packed my kids up and went home to my mom's house she'd have moved heaven and earth to help me. If only I knew then what I know now. We have choices as women, we just need to act on them. It was my fear of what others would think – not of myself but of him – that's pretty screwed up!

I'm pretty sure that one or more of my daughters have been in similar situations and they've not reached out for help either. This is a cycle that needs to be broken. We've got to be there for our daughters. We've got to let them know that, no matter what, home is a safe spot, a place to rest and get their bearings because they are worth more than what they endure. And that goes for our sons as well. They are not exempt from the pain that a dysfunctional marriage can sometimes bring.

I had choices, but it didn't even occur to me that I could get out of that bad situation. I could have spared myself a lot.

DREAM JOB

In the summer of 1985 I got hired at the AMC plant here in Toledo, Ohio, to build the iconic Jeep. The starting wage was $11.07 an hour and I said a very happy goodbye to the part of me that had been working as a waitress all these years getting nickel and dimed to death. I could not have been any happier.

I started in the paint shop and it was a brand new state of the art building and it was the reason for them having to do a massive hiring of like 900 people.

On day one I met Chris Villegas another little Mexican woman – and I mean little she was about 4 feet tall – and we hit it off. We worked together sanding those cars like nobody's business. We came out of there with sand in our noses, all over our faces, and our clothes covered with sand. Apparently we were over-sanding, but nobody told us any different. We worked in a sanding booth and a guy who was in there with us would play a radio all night and we would just sing to the radio and that was how we got through the nights. Oh gosh I gotta laugh at how hard we worked in the early days. We wanted to make a good impression as we were on a 30 day probation period and then after the 30 days we would be in the union.

I'll never forget on our 30th day we were late. I overslept and I was late picking up Chris. She didn't drive at all at the time so I found myself giving her rides every day, which I didn't mind. It took away some of the nervousness of working in the factory which I'd never done in my life. At least it gave me someone to share it with. So I told Chris that instead of punching the time clock we could tell them that we'd forgotten and then they wouldn't be able to tell what time we got there. We could hear the bell ringing from outside the building. As luck would have it, the line was down and no cars were being built so we didn't miss anything.

It worked absolutely like nothing I'd ever known. The line ran nonstop except for our lunch breaks and the team leader would come around to each person to relieve them from their job for 10 minutes. You were then able to go out to smoke or to use the bathroom, but you couldn't do both. No smoking was allowed in the paint shop for obvious reasons and 10 minutes went fast!

I don't know how I made it in those early years. Rose was seven, Ann was four years old, and Junior was just 16 months old.

It wasn't long before we were getting bumped out of our department and having to go to different buildings and doing different jobs. We went together, Chris and I, most of the time because we had the same seniority so that was good because we'd become good friends and partners in crime. The place was a cesspool, I quickly learned that what happened at Jeep stays at Jeep, yeah that's right – just like Vegas. The place is locked down with no outsiders allowed and you're spending time with your coworkers more than you are at home with your spouse and so it's easy to get attached, and to confide all sorts of things in your coworkers both male and female and they know pretty much all your business. Affairs were a large part of the daily goings on. It was referred to as someone having a Jeep wife or Jeep husband. And it could go on for a long, long time. And some people on the outside knew about it because it caused lots of divorces.

Workers would come in hungover or even drunk from the night before. I watched a guy do coke right on the line. It was unbelievable. I actually questioned myself if he really just did that? To which I answered, " yes he did." It was very much culture shock and I learned real quick to adapt. It wasn't long before I was going out to lunch at the Post that was right across the street. You had just enough time to get through the gate, go and guzzle one or two beers and get back to the line before the bell rang. You could even get in your car and drive a block or or two depending on who you were going with and if you had a parking space in the front of the lot.

Some remained in their cars and drank beer from coolers they brought from home. I did that too on occasion. It wasn't bad until I started going out after work, that's when I started getting into trouble...

Jeep sisters
Maggie, Chris, and Rachel

First Separation

I was staying out too late and of course it was causing problems in my marriage. I began an affair with a coworker. I had been unhappy for a very long time when I met Paul and he made me laugh. I just wanted to be with him more. We started talking on the phone outside of work and one day Lee came to me and showed me papers he'd filed with the court stating that I needed to vacate the house. It was an emergency order granting him temporary custody of the kids and I couldn't take anything with me but my clothes and any tools of my trade.

I was in disbelief and quite embarrassed of course and the fact that he had some sort of recording device on the phone and heard my conversations just told me that that was it for my marriage. It had finally come to the end and in the most disgraceful way.

I packed my clothes and went to Tia Lupe's house and she invited me to sleep on her sofa for as long as I needed.

It was a miserable time. I continued to work and Lee got a neighbor lady across the street to watch the kids while he worked and I was only able to see them every other weekend. They were so little and didn't understand what was happening. I quickly fell into depression and didn't know what to do with myself. I continued to drink and feel sorry for myself even though I was the one who had created the mess. Lee's family knew about it, my family knew about it, and there was no saving face. I spent Christmas and New

Year's without my kids. I missed them so badly. I hated to be away from them – Lee knew that and asked me if I wanted to come back home. He'd filed for a divorce already and the day before we were expected to go to court I moved back in.

We never contacted the attorney to tell them and so we had to pay for a divorce that we never got.

But nothing changed. I was still so unhappy and now dealing with depression and having to work alongside Paul for some time.

It was bad making that decision to come back. All we did was argue, ugly, in your face, name calling accusations ugly. We couldn't go anywhere where we'd have even just a drink that didn't lead to an argument or him getting jealous.

We went to a gathering that his brother Roger and my friend Marsha had at her mother's house after they got married downtown. We hadn't been there a half hour and he started to give me the evil eye and I walked out. I walked down the road and was picked up by some guy who was driving and he must've thought I looked distressed because he asked me if I needed a ride and without thinking, I jumped into his car. I don't even know to this day if Lee ever came looking for me.

I went with this guy, this stranger, to a party in the woods. Somewhere in West Toledo some rich kid was having a party and that is where we ended up. Afterwards he took me and drove me to Tia Lupe's house where I stayed the night. I can't even believe that that was my life. I mean, who does that? Go with a stranger? It was such a reckless thing to do. That stranger could have been a killer. The kids were staying with my mom for the night, and I felt free to do what I wanted, but getting together with a stranger because I was hiding from my husband was not the best choice.

And this kind of behavior was just the beginning of how the remainder of our marriage was going to be. I started to think he allowed me to come back home to him and the kids just so he could continue to verbally abuse me, and throw every single thing I'd done in my face time and time again.

Actually I truly believed that he invited me to come back home because he loved me and despite all the anger he was feeling about everything and the way it went down, he still wanted to be with me. Yet he couldn't get it out of his head, the betrayal that was much bigger than he was able and willing to live with.

He would refer to me as "You People." I kinda laugh at that today because it was like we, my family, all grouped together, were from some alien planet but in actuality he was referring to us as Mexicans which to him was derogatory.

I wish I had a dollar for every time he told me that if it weren't for him I'd be in a gutter somewhere. I actually believed it at one time. My self esteem was so low no matter how much I tried.

I always took pride in my appearance, my home, and my work performance. I took care of my children and I was good to my husband. But he talked to me like he was better than me and like I should be indebted to him for even being with me. Like I was the lucky one.

Wait a minute... YOU pursued ME. I was happy before you came into the picture.

All the while I was sharing my blessings with him. Our home, money mom would give us when we needed a helping hand, my job, my friends, my family. And he would joke around with them like he hadn't just referred to us as you people.

Moving To A New House

When Mom purchased the house on South Street, she paid a $10,000 down payment that she got from the sale of the bungalow where I'd grown up. She was pretty well set with her Railroad Retirement pension; her house payment was $227 a month, including taxes and insurance, but she was terrible at managing her money and since she'd given up drinking she started abusing pills such as Valium and Darvocet.

Briefly she had a new boyfriend who moved into the house with her. He had a couple of kids, so she went through her money every month really quickly, and then when she got tired and sent him packing, she got a new boyfriend. But this one had his own house and so she started spending all her time there and not making her own house payment and soon she was being threatened with foreclosure.

She'd fallen terribly behind to the tune of $2,000 and I convinced her to sign the house over to me so that I could get a loan and pay the arrearage and save the house. Reluctantly she did. She didn't want to but I told her I was not going to give her the money just to watch it happen again and I needed a home for my children.

The house had come to need some repairs and she was unable to do them and didn't want to pay out any money.

Working at Jeep afforded me the opportunity to take out a loan at the Credit Union to bring the house payments up to date and it became ours. Lee and I were homeowners again. Even though I'd already lived there before, I loved that the house was big – two stories with three bedroom and a full basement which gave all the kids plenty of space – and beautiful and in a very nice neighborhood. It had a fenced yard both in the front and back and front porch that ran the length of the house where we sat many nights just watching the traffic. On occasion someone we knew would drive by and honk their horn. We put a pool up for the kids.

It became a place for the family to gather and have dinner and celebrate birthdays and all the cousins could bring their kids and they could all swim together. We held a wedding reception there for Angie and her then husband Jerry. All the kids were baptized while we lived there and afterward invited all the family to celebrate. There was plenty of room for everyone and the kids started school in the same school that their dad and I both attended, just one block away.

Working at Jeep was a blessing for me. It meant food always in the house, the kids had nice clothes, and great Christmases. We went to Cedar Point amusement park in Sandusky, Ohio, every year and we took vacations to Tennessee where Lee's parents retired.

Mom didn't remain with her friend for very long and soon found herself homeless. She chose to be with a younger guy who lived with his mom and then wanted to bring him into the home, what was her home but now was mine. It became a real battle for me because I found myself always stuck in the middle of problems between her and Lee.

She had a camper in the back yard and wanted to stay in that and I didn't think it was a problem, but Lee did. Then at one time she had a dog and Lee didn't want it in the house and she wouldn't come in without it. A few times I found her sleeping on the front porch. It was always something and I was always the bad guy. I didn't tell her that Lee didn't want her sleeping in the camper. I didn't tell her that Lee didn't want the dog in the house, trying to save face and not wanting him to look bad. I was acting as if it was me laying down the law. It made her resent me. I could see it in her face when she would look at me, in disbelief and hurt. And I remained stone cold. It was the only way I could cope with either one of them.

After Mom signed over the house to us she would find it necessary to then throw it in our faces and I guess that's where Lee had a problem. But I could see it from her point of view as well and maybe she was being a little harsh, but I'm sure she lived with many regrets and that was probably a big one. I mean, after all, with a house payment of $227, she would pay a phone bill of hundreds of dollars but not make the house payment. She would buy pills before she bought food. Her health was deteriorating and I was really concerned.

At one point, when she was in her 50s, she said she was pregnant. Come to find out she really wasn't.

Once in the middle of a big blowout we were having, Lee alluded to having slept with her adding also, " it was good too!" I know my eyes got big as quarters and he immediately had that look on his face in response to my look, that he shouldn't have gone there. But it was too late and even though he later said it wasn't true it always left doubt in my mind I believed that it could very well be true. I'm pretty sure I chased him through the house that day trying to kill him! It's a terrible thing to have to live with and my way of coping was just to work hard, take care of my family the best I could, and drink in my waking hours because then I just didn't care.

The silent treatment came in very handy during those days. I went about my business on a daily basis as if he didn't even exist, I would look right through him and it was fairly easy. It helped that I had a job working so many hours and we worked opposite shifts of one another.

These were very trying times both mentally and physically.

Scottie continued living there with us and was a real big help with the kids. I was laid off after a while but Lee continued to work and making that house payment was never an issue.

I took a job out of state after a while. I was able to go work as a preferential hire at the Jeep plant in Kenosha, Wisconsin. A lot of their workers had come to Toledo when they got laid off from their jobs and they decided to stay. So then that opened up positions that needed filling until they hired replacements. It was a temporary thing but lasted longer than it was supposed to.

I moved in with about five others. We shared all expenses renting a townhouse. Angie was there also as she'd been hired at Jeep as well, though she didn't remain long before she got sick and had to return home.

We shared a room where we slept on the floor. Once she was gone I was the only one in the house who worked the second shift. The workdays were long – 10 hour shifts – and I slept most of the time when I wasn't working. That was pretty much all I did and every third weekend I would drive home and stay a day and a half then turn around and go back for another three weeks. Lee visited me one time while I was there. I was so lonely I missed my family so much.

I was never so happy to receive a pink slip several months later. I packed up my car so fast I never even told anyone I was coming home. I just got on the road wanting to surprise them.

The entire time that I was working, I sent all my money home. I lived on $100 a week. Lee took the money and the opportunity to remodel the entire kitchen and he and his brother-in-law did a great job, I was very happy with it.

Rachel Clark, Kenosha, Wisconsin, 1987

Lesson 2
Forgive Quicker

The sooner you can cut off that ball and chain, or drop that sack of rocks you've been carrying around with you, the better you'll feel. It's life changing to forgive. You'll be able to breathe again and won't catch yourself holding your breath as much. You'll walk upright without pain and your smiles and laughter will be genuine again.

You'll simply be a much happier person. As God intended you and me to me.

Once I learned to do all that I could and allow God to do the rest it made for a whole new lifestyle.

I didn't worry about what happened, or what might happen because it was, needless to say, wasteful! But I knew that God would work out everything for me that I couldn't work out for myself.

But in order to be able to live in such a way I needed to forgive, just as He had forgiven me.

It's not an easy thing to do. Sometimes I feel the tension instantly in my neck (hence pain in the neck) when I reminisce about certain things. How many know that's a real thing?

I have to speak forgiveness out loud, "I forgive that. Do it as often as you need to and it may be several times."

Hey, I'm only human, too, and sometimes I question if I've really actually forgiven things or instances because I divert back to the feelings of anger. But when that happens I have to remind myself that what I'm actually feeling is the hurt. Because sometimes battle wounds hurt for a long time before they turn into scars.

ANOTHER BABY

It wasn't long before I returned home that I was expecting again with my fourth child. Baby Marie was born in the very hot summer of 1988, on July 29.

Lee hung sheets from the entry ways so that we could all be in the living room where the only air conditioner was situated in a window. One day there was a knock on the door and it was the Mormon guys who went around on their bikes offering Bible tracts about salvation. I invited them in because I was just in that kind of mood I guess where I wanted to hear what they had to say. Unlike Jehovah Witnesses, Mormon believe that all humans are God's children, like Jesus Christ who they know as Jehovah.

Jehovah's Witnesses believe that the only God is Jehovah, whose only son is Jesus and Jehovah created all human beings. They consider Jesus as less than God. It's kinda confusing, especially to me having been raised and growing up Catholic.

I recall one trip we made to Tennessee. My mom had given me an 8x10 inch framed photograph of the Pope to take down to Lee's grandma who was sickly and elderly. He let me take that all the way down to her and I gave it to his mom where she graciously accepted it and placed it on her dresser. On our way home, Lee said it would be taken down because they were Pentecost and didn't believe in the Pope. I hadn't even considered that. That's how much I knew about religion, but I was on a quest to learn and have a more spiritual understanding of things. I was raised traditionally Catholic, which includes attending Catholic services on Sundays. I would take my kids at 11:30 AM because it was the later of the two services. It was in Spanish and the only one who understood what was being said was yours truly. My kids didn't speak a bit of Spanish, but they knew the rituals – stand up, sit down, kneel, up again, in between readings, and the receiving the bread which we didn't do because you had to confess first and we never did that. It was just my way of going through the motions and trying to do what I thought was right and what was expected of me being a mom.

The Mormons were very nice, and sincere. I remember the other kids who were in the living room with me. They talked to them as well as congratulated me on the birth of Marie. They didn't want to take up much of my time after they saw us all in the living room like that and I appreciated it. I shared with them about being in the Catholic Church.

Another visitor I had around that same time was Kara, a grade school friend who was a very big part of my life growing up. Years ago, she and Angie had snuck out of the house even after I warned them not to for fear of them getting caught, which they did. They were riding around with Kara's then boyfriend Bobbie Pratt in a stolen vehicle. Of course he didn't tell them that it was stolen, they had to find out the hard way.

Earlier in the day he'd given Mom a ride home from the grocery store so she wouldn't have to wait for a cab. And now she was having to take a cab to go downtown to pick up Angie where she and Kara were being held until a parent came to pick them up. According to Mom that was punishment enough for Angie. Kara was grounded for weeks. Kara lived with both her mom and dad; she was their youngest.

This time... Kara was coming to tell me that she'd just lost her mom to cancer. I knew they'd been very close. Kara had gone into the Army and came back a different person than who I remembered. Kara told me the doctors used their mom as an experiment like a guinea pig, she was so angry about it and I hated seeing her so upset. In the end her mom passed anyway and she swore she would never let them do that to her.

I wouldn't see her again for many years and then I caught a glimpse of her dancing out on the dance floor of the casino all by herself. She was oblivious to anyone around her and I even called out to her several times and she never heard me. I had to wait for her to come off the dance floor to be able to talk to her. She was quite inebriated and proceeded to tell me that she'd just lost her dad.

As teenagers her brother was killed in a car accident coming home from a concert with a friend. They had been drinking and wrapped the car around the telephone pole, it affected Kara greatly. The friend who was in the car with her brother survived, and out of some kind of loyalty she began a relationship with him that was abusive and she remained in that situation for much longer then she should have.

Since I was laid off from my job at the time, I started selling Home Interior and Gifts just to pick up a little money, well that was the plan. I actually spent more money on buying things for the home and giving things away than I ever earned.

Home Interiors and Gifts is a direct sale company with products such as framed art and candles, mirrors, shelves, wall sconces, figurines, and many more items for the home. I took a few classes on how to arrange certain things on an easel that represents the walls of the home and then I would go into the home and demonstrate how you could beautify your walls and give tips and sell these items to ladies who the host would invite and get more parties booked from them. I learned a lot about direct selling. It was short lived. Although I really enjoyed the idea behind it, I kinda slacked off. And I was nervous to get up in front of people to demonstrate and so I would drink a few beers to relax a little before the parties and someone mentioned that to my recruiter and she mentioned it to me. I played it off by playing dumb but I'm pretty sure she knew it was probably true.

The recruiter happened to be a family friend but still she was very successful in the business and I'm sure she didn't appreciate being told this about one of her workers. The main reason for my selling in the first place was to be able to purchase things for my home at a discount and earn gift items as well. It was a very popular home decor line at the time and I did get many nice things for our home and for my mom as well.

They had this statue of a Cocker Spaniel that you could sit on the floor and it was life-like and it reminded me of our Cocker Spaniel at the time, Benny. I had bought one for myself and thought it'd be nice to buy one for Mom. So I got the box with the statue sealed in it and the kids and I drove over to Mom's to surprise her with it. The few beers I had helped add to my excitement to give it to her. The kids and I arrived all excited that we had a surprise for her. We told her that it was a puppy and we're all really giddy about it. And so I show her this box and it's all sealed and she gasps and can't believe I have this poor puppy in a sealed box and is urging me to hurry and open it and is fearful that this puppy isn't going to be alive and so the kids and I continue to make light of it all and when I finally rip open the box and pull the dog out she just held her chest tight in relief that it was a statue of a puppy and not a real puppy.

After a while I took a job as a waitress. This time at Uncle John's Pancake house. One of my mom's very good friends had a daughter who worked there and she told my mom that they were hiring. It was clear across town but I really liked it and didn't mind the drive. It was fast paced and I could get in and get out early with decent tips every day. You want to work the morning shift at a pancake house. On a Sunday I could make $100 in tips. It was the first time I'd ever made tips like that.

One day a Jeep worker came in there who I recognized and he told me about the Jefferson North Assembly Plant in Detroit, Michigan, taking preferential hires. Jeep had been bought by Chrysler so it was now Chrysler Jeep. They had built a billion dollar plant – all state-of-the-art equipment and they were building the Grand Cherokees at Jefferson North in Detroit Michigan.

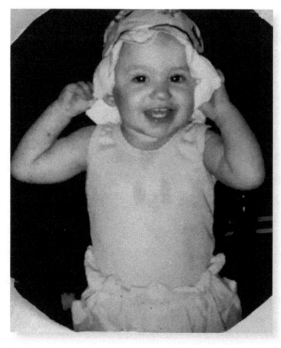

Baby Marie at the South Street house, 1989

GOING TO WORK IN DETROIT

Out of all of the Chrysler plants this one had the oldest work force and these people were being worked to death, literally. They were on a 10 hours, six days a week schedule, with every two weeks a Saturday off. And they wanted to run this way on three shifts. So they were taking all laid off workers first from any other Chrysler plants before they hired off the street. With Detroit being only an hour away it was a no brainer. They had people there from Belvedere, St. Louis, Kenosha, Wisconsin, and quite a few from Toledo, Ohio, where I was from.

It didn't take long to get all my papers filled out to go to Jefferson North. I was able to get on a vanpool that met at a Meijer on Alexis Road in West Toledo so I didn't even have to worry about driving. Although I did just a few times when I missed the van or had to drive because I needed to leave work early for some reason. It was a total culture shock for me. First time ever meeting a woman who had been a man. She was in charge of the Toledo People, and had to put us in hotels a couple times when the weather was too bad to travel home because of ice or snow. Working nights we didn't even get off until 2 AM then we had another hour of travel time.

By culture shock I mean that I had come from a plant where there were about 10% African Americans to a plant where there were 90% African American, the food available was different, the music they listened to throughout the plant was different, and they danced and had fun on the job unlike anything I'd seen before.

But with all that money they were making came some bad as well. There were drugs in the plant, people throwing up the garbage cans, coming in so high, and performing their jobs very poorly to say the least. In my van pool there was one guy who got into drugs really quickly and would always be asking us for five dollars or even just one dollar. By the time he got his paycheck he owed it all to the drug man who was in the plant.

It was no secret that all the long hours were taking a toll on all of us who were making the trek from Ohio. We didn't have to go far but in total from the time I left my house and made it back again I'd been gone 14 hours. 10 hours actually working, two hours travel time back and forth to the meeting site, and then two more hours travel time back and forth to work. During the winter months it took even longer due to snow and ice. It was just a matter of weeks and we were feeling the effects. Everybody was asking everybody if they were alright? "You alright?" "Yeah, man I'm alright." "You alright?" "Yea, I'm alright too." It was a daily thing. The van we rode in was a nine passenger van, but we had seven passengers because we wanted a little extra room and not be packed in like sardines. On occasion we had an extra person who was waiting to get into another van pool.

Our van driver had been a truck driver so he had good experience and handled our van with no problems whatsoever. Even still being on the road so often made me feel uneasy. Cars traveled so fast and there were always accidents on the Interstate.

Even though I was working so late into the evening, I could not go right to sleep when I got home, I was too wired. So I would drink a few beers and go to sleep sometime around 4 or 5 AM. Lee got the kids off to school in the morning except the baby Marie who was four at the time and I would have to get up and take care of her. It was exhausting. I had no idea that it was going to be so hard. I became really depressed and had to see my doctor about going on a stress leave. I was able to take two weeks off and she put me on a medication called Paxil and told me that it was just a mood enhancer. I wouldn't even know I was on anything. That first week that I was off I was like a zombie. I remember it clearly. I would catch myself just staring into space unable to even move. I had no desire to even open my mouth to speak but I had to force myself. I had kids to take care of. I'd gotten a good taste of what depression felt like.

All the times I would tell my mom who had bouts of depression to snap out of it, well I was taking that all back now. I know what it feels like and you can't just snap out of it. By the time the meds kicked in and I started to feel human again, I had to really consider how and if I was going to be able to continue down this path. I'd heard some of my coworkers were looking into moving either into Detroit or somewhere between home, Toledo, and Detroit. That wasn't an option for me to just sell my house and move. Then I'd also heard that some were looking into possibly returning to our home plant. Detroit had said that they didn't pay us for three weeks of classroom training just to let us come back home. But our seniority was back to work again in Toledo. It became a real dilemma. I talked about it with Lee and he was pretty adamant about my staying in Detroit and that there was always a chance of getting laid off again if I returned home. But that was a chance I was willing to take because I just couldn't see me doing this commute for any longer then I absolutely had too.

I burned out fast. I started missing work. I was drinking more and more and the pills weren't helping. I was angry with my situation and angry with Lee for even suggesting that I continued working in Detroit. He knew first hand how I was struggling. It caused me to really resent him and we fought lots! It got so bad that he left and went to his dad's and was prepared to stay in his basement. He wasn't gone one night and I thought I was having a nervous breakdown and begged him to come home. It was the effects of the alcohol and my mental state that I couldn't live with him and I couldn't live without him.

Junior age 4, Rose age 10,
Ann age 8, Marie age 8 months

DRINKING DRINKING DRINKING

I had always been a happy-go-lucky drinker and drunk, but when we drank together Lee would start shit and was relentless to the point I would chase him through the house wanting to kill him. And he would laugh at me and call me crazy and I was! I was like a wild woman, no longer a happy drunk. Those days were over and I was trying to survive, but his behavior changed, too, and I believe he thought he could do almost anything he wanted and I would still want to be with him. And why would he think anything different? By my actions up to that point he could have.

We didn't spend any time together until the weekends when I didn't have to work and if I wasn't giving him the silent treatment, we were probably fighting. Usually it was over stupid shit. Once he kept turning off the light in the dining room where I was trying to do something and when I kept turning it back on he got up on a chair to take the bulb out and I proceeded to pull the chair out from under him. He was a big guy and wasn't going anywhere. He started to get a little rough with me so I called the police on him.

When they arrived he told them about me trying to pull the chair out from him and they looked at him like he was freaking nuts. Yeah, that kind of game playing is what we had arrived at. Just anything to make each other miserable. Looking back now it's almost comical – had it not been for thoughts of ending my life and just calling it quits for real it would be – but I was hurting for real and didn't know how to express myself in a positive way and neither did he. And I knew the drinking was getting worse but I couldn't stop that either.

We had taken a weekend trip to Tennessee to visit his parents and I was worried about having to go the entire time with no beer. That's when I told myself that I had a problem. Up to that point I had been drinking everyday – going to bed with a beer, drinking and driving with the kids in the car, making Jell-O shots for my van pool, having beer in the car when I went anywhere, sending the kids into the house to get the beer I've forgotten, cooking, doing laundry, cleaning the house, even going to school events all while drinking.

I started to notice it affecting me mentally. I was driving through downtown Toledo and stopped at a red light when I got this sudden image flash in front of me of my two older girls laying in caskets side by side. It was close to Christmas and I had bought them nameplate necklaces as one of their gifts and in the caskets where they were laying they were wearing the necklace and the outfits each was wearing was from their actual wardrobe. I was in a state of shock, like did that really just happen? And where did it come from? I'd never experienced anything like that before. It moved me to seek counseling for the entire family.

I had some really great insurance that covered mental illness and so finding a family therapist was really very easy. We had a few in the network and I chose a woman, well that didn't go over well with Lee and he refused to go to the first couple of sessions, so I went alone. We touched on so many unresolved issues from my childhood. As an alcoholic daughter of an alcoholic, there was plenty to talk about right there. Lee did end up at one session, but it was a disaster.

I discussed with Ann all the things that had been happening up to that point – home, life, job, and drinking. I told her about the flash of the image with my girls laying the caskets. I told her about the sudden feeling of impending doom I would get while working on the line and how I felt I needed to get to a phone to call home and make sure everything was alright. And how if nobody answered the phone I start to think the worst and believe that maybe my family had been in a car accident or something. I told her about always being in the middle of Mom and Lee's issues. How unhappy I was and she agreed I'd had a lot going on. She told me that working away from home was just giving me anxiety and that whatever was going to happen was going to happen if I worked out of town or I worked in town. It was like a light switch came on and just that one thing alone was worth the session. I told her about coming back home to Toledo to work and that decision was really weighing heavy on me.

One day I was coming home and happy with the decision and then the next day I was staying in Detroit and happy with that decision it was driving me nuts, I gave her an ear full and they were only hour-long sessions. So after a couple of sessions she brought Lee in and and he told Ann that my mom had told our oldest daughter about him having denied her as a baby, which she did, and how he felt their relationship had been strained since then and he resented my mom for it and it was very difficult for him to get past it. I understood his position, as I had also been very angry when I found out Mom had told Rose that. She had no reason for having done it either and was unapologetic about it. So we both had valid issues and we both wanted to be right and he denied some things I brought up and the counseling was a wash – we never went back.

We found out that the company was in fact going to allow us, all of the preferential hires, a one time chance to return to our home plants. I guess people raised enough stink that the company just wanted to be done with us. We had a window coming up and I needed to make my decision very soon.

Something happened that made me question my sanity during that time. There may be a couple of things that you may find very hard to believe, and trust me, I've questioned them myself over the years.

I was working the line one night and I was playing in my head over and over what to do? I'd gotten into a fight with Lee and told Rose that we were moving out of the house. I was packing up and leaving and we were going to start over in a new place! I'd had enough of her dad and all the fighting. She was happy as could be, happy to be getting away from all the yelling and fighting and then I changed my mind. Because I'd be leaving all my support system and then I'd have no one near me to help with the kids. It crushed her. I could not keep doing this to my kids.

So this was playing in my head as I was installing mirrors on a Jeep Grand Cherokee when all of a sudden everything went quiet. I could see people's lips moving but I couldn't hear them talking. I could see they were laughing, but I couldn't hear them laughing. I couldn't hear the radio playing. It was dead silent.

Then all of a sudden I heard a woman's voice in my ear say, "You're going home." And I felt this incredible feeling of warmth run through my body.

As soon as she said that, all the noises could be heard again. Every time I tell this story it makes me so emotional because as hard as it is to believe I know that it's true. Because of the overwhelming feeling that I got when it happened 29 years ago and today, as I write this with tears streaming down my face, as God is my witness, it happened just that way. I went home that night and told Lee about it. I told him that an angel had spoken to me and told me that I was coming home. This started a real fascination with angels for me. I'd always believed in them and that they are with us always but don't make themselves known because then we would start to worship them.

I purchased a couple of books on stories about angels. I just wanted to know more. But let me tell you how my mind worked okay because it wasn't enough that an angel, I call her my Detroit angel, spoke to me but the following week I was heading to the office to sign papers to remain in Detroit. Yes, to remain in Detroit. As I approached the counter I could see a woman sitting behind a glass window. I was nearly at the window, and something made me turn slightly and walk right past it. Did that just happen? I questioned myself. Why did I just walk past that window? I honestly felt like something turned me, not physically. I didn't feel anything touch me but I sensed being turned away from that window and I never missed a beat. I just returned to my job once again questioning my sanity.

Was I stupid or what, what was it going to take? That's what drinking was doing to me. I couldn't even make a decision. Every day that I traveled to Detroit now by this time it had been very close to a year, maybe about 10 months of being on this vanpool I had great anxiety about being on the road. I felt like I was going to die on the road by being in an accident.

We had a guy in our vanpool temporarily, I don't remember why or even how long he rode with us, but one day as I was getting on he was already seated in the last row where I was heading also. He looked up at me and said "man, you're yellow" and gave me a forced grin and was shaking his head back and forth. And I told him that when I woke up that morning and I looked in the mirror that I thought I looked yellow. First time ever! I didn't know what to think. I'd never been yellow before and I didn't even associate it at the time with drinking. He told me that he'd been in AA for some time and left it at that. It's the only time I remember looking yellow like that. It's not something that ever happened again.

Rose, Joyce seated was the foster child who used to babysit them, Ann, and Junior

L-R Ann and Rose at
South Street house

No Love No Respect

I didn't really need another reason for my return home, but Lee gave me one when he was fired from his job where he worked at a large box store as an appliance repairman.

I was working so much overtime that we were able to pay cash for new living room furniture, we purchased a sofa, a loveseat, a chair, even lamps, and end tables. It was the first time I'd ever been able to buy brand new furniture. And it was all paid in full within two weeks. Though we received our discount, he returned to the store the following week and said some bullshit story about not getting it. The next thing I knew, he was fired. I was in complete disbelief and embarrassed for him. And now he'd lost his job over something so stupid and I could not ever understand why he did it.

I felt so disrespected. Like here I am, busting my ass working all these hours and it just isn't enough? Would it ever really be enough? I was struggling mentally and physically and I felt myself going down and down and I felt as if I was heading for a nervous breakdown and was on the edge and going over any moment. I was just holding on by a thin thread. And he couldn't explain to me why he did it. I can only imagine that it was out of greed.

He wasn't out of work for very long; he never was, that wasn't an issue. He was an excellent provider – he worked hard, he was a good tentative father, he made sure that I had everything I needed, like cigarettes for work and coffee. He would buy me snacks and start my car on cold mornings to clean the snow off.

Something may have seemed small, but he did so many things for our family. He cooked, cleaned, and took us on vacation every year. We visited family and family visited us. Nobody saw the man that he was turning into in the last few months we were together. And it wasn't really him as a person, but more so his behavior. He was going through some stuff, as well as I clearly was, and neither of us could help the other. Of course I can't speak for him and it was only years later that I began to suspect this, but I want to believe that it's the truth.

I suspect that it might have something to do with the porn that I found in the basement one day. I was livid. I'm also a very big prude! What is a prude? According to the Dictionary: a person who is or claims to be easily shocked by matters relating to sex or nudity.

First of all I was upset at having found it because he had it, and second of all I had four kids in the house! Had they seen it? How long could it possibly have been there? I knew instinctively that was the reason he was talking dirty to me all of a sudden. I hated it and he would start as soon as we were in the car alone. I hated to be in the car with him. It was a complete turn off for me, not that I was ever really turned on because let's just be real I wasn't attracted to him in that way. My sexual desire had not come to fruition – call me a late bloomer. And I'd had four kids at this time so I can't explain it, it just was what it was.

We had been out drinking and were supposed to meet up for breakfast after hours with other family members but instead he drove us home. And I was feeling the effects of the alcohol pretty well, but I still wanted to eat. I asked why we were going home and he said that he was going to go downtown to pick up a girl to bring her home so we could all be together. Girl as in prostitute – you talk about someone sobering up fast! I told him if he did he would return to find me gone! No amount of money, not that he was offering any, could have persuaded me differently. When he realized that it was not going to happen he drove us back to have breakfast like nothing ever happened. I just felt like he had no respect for me being the mother of his four children and wanted me to see me be with another woman. I was afraid at that moment that I would do something like that at some point because I was drinking and just wanted to make him happy or that he could possibly set me up to do it. He had told me a few times while in bed that he was somebody else. Of course I'd been drinking. He was trying to convince me that I was in bed with someone other than him.

It was an automatic buzz kill for me. I lost any respect and any loyalty I may have had left for him, just like he didn't have it for me. I was done at this point wondering what was going to come of my life.

THE LAST NINE MONTHS

It's hard to describe my mental state the last nine months of my drinking, I was literally all over the place. Happy one moment, sad the next, every day was different. Alcohol will do that to you. I had feelings of being unworthy and unlovable, being a failure in oh so many different ways. I think I hated men, no I know I hated men!

I'd also had an honest-to-goodness, frank talk with Lee for the first time ever and thought I could finally understand where he was coming from. He confided in me things that happened to him in his childhood and I had empathy for the hurt little boy. I thought it was a big step in the right direction for us and was hoping to see things change, but they didn't. I wanted to be loved in a way that he just couldn't love me or I just had gotten to the point where I couldn't receive it. I think I was broken. I was approaching my rock bottom though I didn't know it at the time. I could barely have a conversation with him that was civil. I had no energy whatsoever to go there. And I know he knew it. One day he came in with a couple of books in hand by the author Max Lacado and a Bible telling me that he was going to change. He was going to start working on himself to work through some trauma and be a better person all around. And I told him that it was great he needed to do that for himself so he could be happy someday. But it wasn't going to be with me and I knew that but I didn't say it out loud.

I'd already determined that a divorce would be in the near future. I just didn't know how or when. There were lots of things to consider, but one thing was for sure that I had an excellent job and that as long as there was a Chrysler Corporation I would have a job no matter if I had to relocate.

I recall one time doing laundry after everyone had gone to bed and I was drinking a few beers and I was watching the movie *Ghost* in between loads, which had been out for a while by this time with Demi Moore and Patrick Swayze. I went downstairs to the basement where the washer and dryer were, and unexpectedly I just began to cry, I was just so touched by that movie. I was in so much pain and ugly crying I'm sure someone can relate to this. I felt the most unloved as I'd ever felt in my life, undeserving of anything good. I just wanted to be loved. I wanted to know that someone could love me like those two loved each other in the movie. It was the first time that I really felt like I wanted something more in my life. I had a small glimpse of finding some meaningful reason to go on after that cry and felt determined to try to find a way to get there. To this day whenever I hear "Unchained Melody" it takes me back to that scene, not the one playing on the television set, but the one that played out in the basement and it still brings tears to my eyes.

Another day I was caught up at the kitchen sink crying over a father that had denied me my whole life! Alcohol will do that to you, you know. Make you long for something you never had. As bad as this was I'm happy to be able to say that it was the one and only time I cried over him. Because I deserved better than that, and I'm not the one who missed out.

I wanted to stop all this pain that I was in and I didn't know how. I'd never read the Bible but I felt the urge to get closer to God. I started out by buying some angel books and trying to understand what part they were playing in my life because of what

I had experienced in Detroit. I knew more than ever that it had happened and I wanted to know more. Being raised traditional Catholic, I had all my kids baptized at the same time, and each had their own set of Godparents. I took them to church and Lee and I had taken them to his family's church which was Pentecost, but something was missing – big time. I started talking more to God. I started praying for something to give but at the same time I started drinking more to numb the pain. I would stop at Ice Cold Beer, a carryout about two blocks from my home on my way home and buy a pint of screwdriver and drink it down before I even got home. It had turned out to be a way of coping because it just kept me mellow and uncaring of my situation regarding my marriage.

Years later I found out about several inappropriate incidents that Lee was involved with, which were a real eye opener for me and impel me to encourage others to have open communication with your children. Let them know it's okay to tell and to ask for help. No matter who it is or what it is. No one should be allowed to touch their bodies.

Back row: L-R Joey, Mom, Sophia, Izzy, Tia Lupe, Connie
Front L-R Mary and Lina

114

THE CHILDREN

At age 14, Rose was your typical teenager, liked to do her makeup and hair, that high poof that was so popular in the 90s – she did her sisters' hair as well, Ann and Marie. We went through Aqua Net hair spray like crazy and I don't understand the hair teasing and pulling necessary to make that hair stand tall, but all the girls were doing it. The bigger and taller the better. After having had a bad junior high school year with bullying and feeling like she never fit in, after leaving all her grade school friends and going to a school where she didn't know anyone. Had we sent her onto the junior high she was supposed to go to things may have turned out different. But she begged to go to Queen of Peace Catholic school and so we gave in and enrolled her and it was the worst thing we could've done. There was so much drama and tears shed, I didn't know how she was going to get through it. And now she wanted to go to a school out of district and it required signing over custody of her to Lee's sister. Reluctantly we did, she'd already been through so much and we wanted to see her graduate, and be able to attend a vocational school during her high school years and it wasn't available where we lived. She wanted to become a cosmetologist and her aunt Molly was willing to help her achieve that. Rose was outgoing and very friendly. I called her my wild child and had been stifled all because of a bunch of mean girls at this Catholic school. It was her time to shine.

Mom and I, with Angie and all the girls, Rose, Ann, Colleen, Selina, and Marie, loved to dance to the music of New Kids On the Block in the living room and just laugh and have a good time. Ricky Van Sheldon Sang the story of my life on the radio, with such songs as "Somebody Lied" and "Life Turned Her Way."

Ann was my little, shy, gentle-natured child. She was a little mother to the smaller kids. Always looking out for them and helping them. She had a giggle that was contagious and talked a mile a minute. But she was developing a sneaky side and the way I could tell was just a look she had where she would just appear to be observing and making mental notes. She liked this little boy who lived next door, he was a couple years older and I noticed one day how comfortable she looked sitting with his arm around her on the back porch and she was only 11. She came to us one day and asked to go to a friend's house who lived on the other side of a six lane highway. We wouldn't allow her to go because we felt crossing was too dangerous. And then one day she did it anyway and I knew right then and there she was going to be the brave and daring one and she did not disappoint. She became known as my little angel with horns, endearingly of course.

Junior was the cutest little boy and all he wanted was to be included, but with three girls he never caught a break. It was always his fault – he took it, he wouldn't give it back, he was splashing, being mouthy, being too loud, eating it all, you name it, and they were blaming him for it! He loved to sit and watch cartoons and was happy with whatever we gave him even a simple meal like a McDonalds Happy Meal. He never complained about anything. Once he bought two padlocks at the Santa Shop in elementary school for a locker his Uncle Jim gave him. And he put Grandpa's clothes (my step dad Phillip) in the box and locked it then he used the other one to lock his boots together. Phillip had retired from his job at the Devilbiss Company in Toledo, Ohio, and made his home in Lewiston, Michigan. He would come back to Toledo about once a month to take care of business or his mother's affairs and would usually stay with us during that time. Junior had a cousin of his spending the night and I guess they just wanted to play a joke. They were in second or third grade.

I tried to pass the time by having fun days with the kids. It was always a full house with their friends there especially on the weekends when they had friends or cousins who would come and stay the night with them. Or they would go to their friend's house. Or we would go and visit family at their houses. I would take Mom a care package like some dinner that I'd cooked that night and maybe a liter of her favorite drink (Pepsi) and a pack or two of cigarettes. She was always happy to see us on her doorstep bearing gifts.

I was constantly multitasking whether it be cooking and talking on the phone or cleaning while picking up after kids – there weren't many quiet moments. And I'd kinda tune out honestly. I'd just be lost in my thoughts, drinking some beer, and that's how I got through most days if I wasn't working.

SEPARATION AND DIVORCE

Had it not been for my job at Jeep, who knows what would've happened to me and my kids. It really was my saving grace. I could leave all my problems outside the gate when I entered the plant for the day. And at that time we had no cell phones. If you wanted to reach anyone inside the plant you had to actually call the office and leave a message and they would in turn get it to you usually through the union steward.

I was really happy at the new plant I'd been sent to. It was referred to as simply the Stickney plant because it was on Stickney Avenue, where we originally built the Wagoneer. The Wrangler and the Dakota Trucks came later. It's what we were building when I walked in the doors for the first time in 1994.

I can't say enough about working an eight hour day after working nine and 10 hour shifts. And then having only a 15 minute drive home I was the happiest I'd been in a long time at work, and boy did I need that! I worked as a floater, which meant I learned several jobs up and down the assembly line in an effort to fill in for workers who were absent, and I loved it. Some jobs were very physical and my whole body after eight hours of trying to be a contortionist hurt most days, but nothing a few beers after work couldn't help. I'd come to be quite a flirt in those days and laughed and smiled my way through many conversations and made lots of new friends, both male and female. Just work friends, really, nothing outside of work, there was no time for that. All of my extra time was spent with family. But I got really good at my job and I was working hard. It was what was getting me through that part of my life.

I would come home and tell Lee about all the men who flirted with me and he'd be so jealous. It caused a lot of arguments between us and in the end I'd feel so depleted of all of my energy, but I would do it again because I liked the reaction I'd get from him. It was my way of getting back at him for wanting me to do some of the things he wanted. I felt like I was getting my revenge and I felt good about it. Not because I loved him at this point in our marriage. There is no more love. And he may not even have loved me anymore at that point. Maybe it was just an ego trip for him. I was making him look bad to people who knew I was married. But it was all innocent at the end of the day everybody went home.

I'd been at the Stickney plant for a few months and one day my team leader came up to me and told me the that the boss wanted to talk to me. It was lunchtime and I was really nervous because I'd never been in any kind of trouble and couldn't imagine why he would want to talk to me. As I approached the area where his desk was I saw all these people standing around and then they started singing happy birthday to me, yeah, it was my birthday and all this had been a surprise put on by my team leader Terry who probably flirted the most with me. He was just a really nice guy and I found out later that he'd taken up a collection of one dollar from everyone on the team to buy me a birthday cake. It was a complete and wonderful surprise that I never saw coming. I didn't know they could find out that it was my birthday.

I was so happy and appreciative that my team had done this for me and I knew I made the right decision about coming back to my home plant. No matter what happened I was home. I had great coworkers, everyone was so friendly and helpful.

DEAN CLARK

I first laid eyes on Dean while I was crossing the lines at Jeep making my way to the restroom. It was only a 15 minute break and I had to have enough time to step outside to smoke a cigarette, too. This bathroom was upstairs, kinda centrally located in the building, but I was working on another team and I was a little further away than usual. Once in the aisle I looked over to the right and saw this guy sitting on a big stock box and he's leaning against a cement post reading the newspaper and eating an apple. For some reason I could not take my eyes off of him and I continued looking at him even as I walked away. No, I didn't recognize him from anywhere. I'd never seen him before or at least I didn't think I had. I'd worked in this area plenty of times and didn't remember ever seeing him.

He was mesmerizing and I'll never forget how I felt seeing him that day for the very first time.

It was like my soul had recognized him, like I'd been looking for him for a very long time and finally there he was! I had found him. I thought about him all evening that night and looked forward to going into work the next day just to be able to see him again.

I loved my job, especially the group of people who I was working with, and that for eight to 10 hours a day I didn't have to worry about how unhappy I was at home. I could just keep pretending with family and friends that everything was beautiful. Even though I was on depression and anxiety meds. But now I had this guy who came out of nowhere who was handsome and

I could look at him and somehow be happy. I didn't understand why, but I was going with it.

And that's what I did for the next couple of weeks. He had no idea that I existed but that was okay.

He came to work everyday wearing a green Army jacket type coat and that was what I watched coming down the aisle, he would be carrying a lunch box and if I missed him I could always look to see if the lunch box was on top of a locker besides his work station. I was a floater. I worked all over the building and so if I got just a glimpse of him in the morning for the day I was happy.

After a couple of weeks I was given a stationary position that just happened to be in the same area and it was off the line, a sub-assembly job. Off the line meaning I was not stuck in an eight foot area and could freely move around. I could go to the bathroom whenever I wanted or step outside for a cigarette. I could run to the canteen for food. It was a job held by a woman of high seniority but the woman had gone out on sick leave and it was offered to me as being the highest floater in the area. It was what's called a gravy job and it gave me a much needed break. My blood pressure had been all out of whack and my doctor was trying to get it under control by adjusting the milligrams of my medicine. I'd had a problem with my blood pressure since getting pregnant at 17 and by the age of 20 I was on medicine daily to control it.

One morning while driving into work I had this sudden numbness and tingle around my mouth and I thought for sure it was due to high blood pressure. Thank God I didn't become a doctor because I would find out years later just what it was.

Some may call it luck but I choose to call it divine intervention that this job happened to be directly across from Mr. Army Jacket himself, Dean Clark.

I remained in the shadows, but not for too long. At first I didn't know how I was going to let him know that I was there, but one day an idea came to me and I was just fixated on it and I needed to act on it right away. The weekend was coming up and I just felt this sudden urgency to make a move, but what was I going to say? It was nearly lunchtime and I was going out for lunch to drink a beer at the corner and I needed to think fast and I just said the first thing that came to me!

He was leaning over his workstation and I got in real close to him and I said "Have I told you lately how handsome you are, and how you excite me so?" Oh my gosh I really said that! (Laughing) He didn't even so much as look up but he replied with, "Nooooo."

I never looked back and I just kept walking out of the plant. I needed to do that before I'd had a beer, I wasn't going to let myself feel like it was the alcohol talking. Now when I came back that was a different story because I'd had alcohol but it didn't matter because Dean never gave me the time of day or even looked in my direction that I know of. And he never did for three days and the weekend came and went and I didn't give it much thought honestly, I was too busy for that. And I was grateful for distractions.

Lee had gotten a new job doing appliance repair and we'd been invited to a cookout by one of his new coworkers. He asked me if I could make taco salad for it and I'd told him no, I think I had a bug up my ass, not sure but I also could have just been really tired. I just didn't want to. It made him angry and so we didn't talk but on the day of the cook out I got up with full intentions of making the taco salad but he was already making it and not speaking to me. Then at the cookout he didn't speak to me – talk about awkwardness. It was an eye opener for me because I was getting the feeling that he'd had it with me, I mean really had it with me. I can honestly say that I'd never gotten that impression before, not like this.

On Monday I went into work so hung over and I was feeling just miserable and couldn't wait for it to finally be lunch time so I could rest my head. As soon as the bell rang that's exactly what I did. I put my head down on my desk. Not long after maybe just a few minutes I heard somebody talking. "Did you really mean what you said to me?"

I was NOT in any way, shape, or form ready to have that conversation that day. But it didn't matter, I had to. I had to open a dialogue ready or not and explain just who I was. Because he didn't know me from Eve. Honestly he didn't know me, maybe he'd caught a glimpse of me walking through the area, he'd given a buck towards a birthday cake for me, he even sang "Happy Birthday" to me, I would later find out, but he didn't know ME. He wanted to know did I mean what I said and why did I say those things to him? Was I joking? Was I playing a joke on him? Were others involved? All I could answer with was a resounding "NO!"

In the ensuing days I spilled my guts out to him. I must've told him my life's story in just a matter of days literally. I mean why not, I felt like I'd known him my whole life and I needed to tell him all that had happened to me and that was happening to me. I told him about the kids and the family and he just listened. I felt like I'd been waiting all my life to find him and I finally had. I wanted him to know that my whole perspective since having laid eyes on him had changed, and that I'd actually felt a glimmer of hope and that I could actually be happy again. I was so grateful for the way he'd made me feel joy in my life again and I wasn't asking him for anything, I just wanted him to know how I was feeling and where I was coming from.

Every single thing that happened after that we did knowingly as adults. It may not have been done in a good or thoughtful way being that both of us were married to others and we had children. But we needed each other and we had to be together. Nothing could've been undone. There was no going back. From that day on, we refer to it as the Great Ice Breaker.

I once referred to it as an emotional affair while talking to Rose, because I just couldn't explain it otherwise. But never once did it occur to me while we were in the throes of it that that's what it was.

We spent the next few weeks just learning about each other. I didn't know what would come of it but I had this feeling that we were supposed to be together. I told him that I didn't want anything from him because I knew he was married with children and then one day he told me that things weren't as they seemed. I remember we were walking outside, within the confines of the plant which is all fenced in and very private. It was a beautiful sunny day in September of 1994 when he told me that it was also the day I found out that his daughter and I shared the same name. My thoughts were all over the place and it was the first time I'd let myself think that we could possibly be together. I even went as far as compiling a What If List.

I thought about Dean day and night, and when I think back to those days, tears come instantly. There is no one who could have gone with me through that time – I'm convinced other than Dean. I do believe that he was and is my soulmate. And that God brought us together for a purpose.

God was able to show me through Dean that there was hope, that I really could be happy and it was an incredible eye opener.

We started taking our conversation outside of the plant by talking on the telephone after work. Which required me to begin sneaking around. I was no longer intimate with Lee because I'd felt like I was being somehow unfaithful to Dean because my heart belonged to him now. My mind was just racing at times because I wondered how I was going to be with him. It was a very unlikely scenario that this was going to be easy considering our situation.

As it turns out things got very ugly. I did leave my home and I moved in with Angie, leaving my children behind. I was in no position to take them with me. I'd been found out and Lee was fighting for custody of them. He would not allow me to take them willingly; he was bound and determined to fight me every step of the way. I knew that I needed to prepare for a long drawn out battle. And so I did.

Dean Clark, 1995

Lesson 3
Consider Collateral Damage

Dean would tell me, "don't sweat the small stuff," and that would raise my blood pressure faster than anything! What seems insignificant is up to the individual. But I will say this about Dean, he can be a little bit too nonchalant at times. Yes there are real situations happening here that must be discussed between us.

I then found that he had a way of calming situations down for me because of that attitude and, like it or not, it worked! Very important in a blended family of yours, mine, and ours.

At times we had to agree to disagree as long as nobody got hurt.

We picked our battles carefully, enough cannot be said about NOT arguing in front of children. They have been through enough just DON'T DO IT!

At times I would have to leave the house because the arguments became so embroiled that I saw no resolution and needed a cooling down period. It's okay to walk away.

It's okay to say nothing at all in an effort to not hurt the other person. Remember that whatever you say you cannot take back no matter what.

GETTING SOBER

First I needed to get sober and I didn't know how I was going to do that.

Dean and I had shared just one drink at one of the bars around the corner from the plant after work one day. It was the only time we ever did.

We met to talk about my situation. I had told him that I was no longer in my home, but staying with my cousin Angie and that my children were with their dad. That I was in search of a good lawyer and that my intent was to quit drinking because it was a problem for me. He didn't know to what extent because he didn't know me. We didn't really know each other, we had just come together under unlikely circumstances.

Sometimes when two people come together for the purpose of emotional needs, things can be easily misconstrued, or embellished. I was telling him my life story about the drinking and fighting Lee and I did for all those years, but he didn't know if I was being honest, I could've been some crazy woman making everything up. And the same could've been true about him. He told me his wife was crazy that she had some mental issues that she had hid from him and I just believed it to be the truth. I later found out that he had in fact left his wife several times in the year and a half that they had been together. Only to return because he wasn't strong enough to stay away, either. And she would guilt trip him into coming back.

Dean was a musician outside of work. He played in a band for many years and met his wife in a bar he played in. I told myself that if he had loved her he would've never given me the time of day, right? I wasn't looking for a Jeep husband as they are sometimes referred to and Dean wasn't looking for a Jeep wife. We wanted to be together but Dean didn't want to hurt his wife. He didn't want to hurt anyone. It was a very hard time for him, but I would've waited for however long it took to be able to be with him.

I went to George's Bar on Broadway in South Toledo one night after work. Regina, the owner and barmaid, a German woman with a very thick accent liked me and she liked my mom and Tia Lupe who had been going there for years. and she would cash my payroll check every Thursday night. Sitting at the bar I ordered a beer contemplating what I was going to do and how much I just wanted to quit drinking and needed to if I was going to be strong enough to get through this divorce and custody battle that I'd be facing in the very near future. The two went hand in hand. The last time I'd left Lee I wasn't strong enough to stay away because I was still drinking and I'd get depressed and start self loathing and just go back like a puppy with her tail between her legs, and Lee liked that control that he had over me while I was drinking. But this time I was not about to let that happen and so I needed to get prepared. But how?

Right there and then, sitting at the bar, I just started praying telling God that I wasn't strong enough to do it on my own and that I was going to need his help. If I was to stop drinking. I felt so defeated and the battle hadn't even started yet.

All of a sudden something just told me to get up and go now! It wasn't an audible voice that I heard but more like an urgent feeling from within but not my own, and I did. I got off that bar stool and left the building.

It was the last drink of alcohol I ever took.

Rachel Clark , 1995

Marie, Rachel, and
Little Rachel

Separation and Divorce Proceedings

I had left my home and had most of my clothes in my car since I'd been staying with Angie. She was nice enough to put me up in her daughter Selina's room for as long as I needed. One of the first nights there I had a nightmare that Lee was chasing me through our neighborhood trying to kill me with a knife. I woke up trying to scream, in my dream I WAS screaming.

I had bouts of insomnia and days where all I wanted to do was sleep. I was going through withdrawals I suppose. I had great anxiety about the future but I wasn't scared one bit. I felt as though God was right there beside me at all times.

By the time I'd gone back home only to retrieve a few more things Lee presented me with an order he'd filed in court, an emergency order granting him temporary custody of the minor children, in it he claimed that I was an alcoholic and on drugs, abusive, was demanding some furniture, and had threatened him with bodily harm.

I was to stay away and only take my clothes and any tools of my trade. I was not allowed to see the children and was not allowed to visit their school at any time. Also included in the order was that I seek treatment for alcohol at a nearby center.

I did not abandon my children. I left them in the care of their dad while I sought help. Yes, it's true that I'd fallen out of love with Lee and no reconciliation was possible and it's true that I'd found someone else who gave me hope and made me feel good about myself and gave me something to look forward to. It is also true that I wanted to be with this new person and I acted hastily without regard for the family. I felt the urge to just flee at the moment and it's what I did. It was a desperate act. Right or wrong, I did it, I left and now I'd have to fight Lee in the courts to get my children back.

It was an ugly scene. I tried to push my way in and Lee wouldn't allow it and caught my hand in the door and broke my finger. Rather to make matters worse I just left and the following week I had an appointment to meet an attorney who came highly recommended by a coworker.

In the afternoon that I met with the attorney it had been a couple weeks since I'd had my last drink. And as I explained to her everything leaving nothing out she complimented me on the fact that I appeared to be bright eyed and she could tell that I'd not been drinking.

Mrs. Amy Berling was her name, attorney at law. I told her about Dean and I told her that Lee knew about Dean, not all the details, but he knew that I'd been talking to another man. On one occasion while Dean and I were talking on the phone, Ann picked up the phone in another part of the house and heard us talking and proceeded to tell her dad that I was talking to another man on the phone. That escalated very quickly and was the reason for my leaving and going to Angie's. We argued and it was the first inclination he had that something was going on.

I was very honest with the lawyer, telling her as much as I could about the current situation and that the most important thing was to be able to establish visitation while we moved forward with a divorce. It had been about four weeks before I was finally able to see the kids. I was granted pretty standard visitation, every other weekend and Wednesdays for a few hours after school.

Marie was only six years old. She was a very happy child, but this changed her. She looked sad and withdrawn like she didn't know how to act around me anymore. She was the baby and everyone, meaning her brother and sisters, treated her as such still and they protected her. Holding her hand as they came and went and engaging in small talk and laughter. They kept it fun both at Angie's house while I was still there and after I'd moved out just a couple of months later.

Dean did leave his wife and my custody battle was, as I knew it would be, long and drawn out and we did everything the wrong way and my children were caught up in it all.

At one time during Thanksgiving of the first year I was Angie's, my children were with their dad, Dean was with his parents with his son Paul who was seven at the time, and his wife was home alone with her son. That's at least four families that were affected by our actions and there was no taking anything back.

Dean and I continued moving forward with our relationship and by Christmas time we rented our first house together, just three months after the Great Ice Breaker.

I do not recommend anybody to do this as it was very hard especially on the children. First Mom and Dad split up, then Mom moves in with another guy we don't even know?! I can't begin to express the guilt I've had over the years for having done to them what I did. There is just no excuse for it. Even over the years I've expressed that I was in a state of mind where I didn't want to live.

How could I even feel like that when I had these beautiful kids? But it was the depression and it was the alcohol that played a big role as well. I loved them! I always loved them and I wanted to be a good mother and I wasn't being one at the time. I was being very selfish both in finding this man to love and tearing their world apart to be with him. The kids were ages 16, 13, 10, and six. It was especially hard on Rose who was not living at home at the time. And she was getting all her information from Lee and his sister Molly, which were usually only half truths.

Junior was showing some signs of aggression at school. Lee pulled him off the sports team for that very reason and he lost his outlet. I don't know if it was the right thing to do but he had friends in the neighborhood who he was in close contact with and I was glad about that.

Ann, who was 13, began acting out in such a way that her dad gladly dropped her off on my doorstep in the middle of the night because he didn't want to be bothered.

It was tough those first few months, maintaining sobriety while all the walls felt like they were closing in on me. Lee was giving me a very hard time, dictating visitation rules.

Dean had custody of his oldest child, an eight year old boy, Paul. My children didn't get along well with him from the very beginning. Paul was used to having his dad to himself and used to his dad doing everything for him and we were just an interruption in his life.

We were a lot and we made a lot of noise and he didn't want to be in a house full of Mexicans is what he told the kids. I never heard him say that to me directly so I'm not sure where it would've come from.

Dean also had a daughter, Little Rachel, and she was seven when we moved in together but she lived with her Mom in Michigan. Dean had regular visitation with her. She was very sweet and all the older kids loved her.

The kids didn't know what to make of their new living arrangements whether it be for the weekend, or for Paul – this was unexpected for him as well. I can't even begin to imagine what was going on in his mind or any of the kids for that matter.

I was newly sober and my kids were not used to that. I was on edge a lot. They couldn't make a lot of noise and they kinda didn't like that too much. I was no longer the fun and happy Mom. I was too uptight now. They didn't know how to act around me anymore. They were just kids and wanted to laugh and have fun.

We were living in a small cottage type house on the water in Point Place, Ohio. It was a small two bedroom with just a living area and kitchen and bath. When the kids spent the night they had to sleep downstairs on the floor.

The walls were so thin and I was later horrified thinking and wondering if the kids ever heard us, Dean and I, in the bedroom. I'm one of the biggest prudes that's ever lived and the thought of that just makes me feel embarrassed to no end. I was thinking one day that probably Ann would've heard something on occasion but I could never bring myself to ask because I'm afraid of what she would say. Dean was and is very loud while making love as he calls it I say having sex, but whatever, he's loud and I'm always having to stifle him. And it never occurred to me in the early days, only years later.

We were only there for a year and then we moved on to a larger home that we purchased in the five corners area of Whitmer High School in Toledo, Ohio.

Everyday that I maintained my sobriety I got stronger and

stronger. I liked the person that I was becoming. I went to work every day and I attended all my court proceedings. I picked up the kids every time I was supposed to and usually had them more than I was supposed to.

One day I had a thought to go to the store and to pick a yellow legal pad and start writing. I took it home and numbered the pages for how many days there were in the month and started to record all the days that I had the kids. On holidays that they were supposed to be with Dad, every weekend that they were supposed to be with Dad but spent it with me, summer vacation... I was filling up the notebook. I was going to show the court that Lee didn't want the kids as he was saying he did, what he wanted was the child support. He'd found a girlfriend and was spending a lot of time with her which was fine with me, but I needed to document and show in court.

Lee wrote me a note one day and sent it with the kids. He was unhappy that I'd taken Marie to get her pictures taken and Ann had put a little makeup on her just to make her happy. She was so excited and we all thought she looked so beautiful and she was the happiest I'd seen her in a long time. It was Easter and she got her picture taken with a rabbit, a real rabbit and the pictures were so cute. I bought them and sent one to Lee's parents and they rejected them and sent them back. They said it didn't look like her and that they didn't approve of her wearing makeup because she was just a little girl. It hurt my feelings so bad because it hurt her. During this same time period, Lee told me that Marie told him that I was questioning her on where she wanted to live. I can't imagine having asked her that; maybe the older kids were questioning her. I didn't want to question her on if she had said that to her dad for all I know he could have been making it all up. But I wasn't going to make things worse for her if she really felt that way – that I was trying to make her pick between me and her dad. He told Marie once to pack her bags and call me to come pick her up, she was coming to live with me. Then before I could get there he'd changed his mind. He was just playing mind games.

I was willing to let the courts decide.

I even thought that I could allow the kids to remain with their dad if that would make them happy. I was so conflicted and I just wanted to do what was best for them. I'd already caused them enough pain.

That was until Lee pulled a fast one and moved the entire family 40 miles away to another town without telling me first or getting permission from the court. He'd met a woman, Carrie, and she was from a small town called Clyde, Ohio, and they thought it'd be good for them to move there and rent out the marital home.

I changed my mind really quickly. He'd already been uncooperative as far as doctor appointments and taking the kids to see a counselor that he'd told the courts he would do and was not. They were supposed to see the counselor who we had seen once as a family. He wasn't informing me of anything that had to do with school. No parent teacher conferences. This included receiving any school pictures. I was livid.

We motioned the court immediately for a change in custody. This in no way affected our divorce proceedings that continued, but a guardian ad litem was assigned to our case and an investigation was set in motion.

Losing My Stepdad Phillip

I lost my stepdad Phillip, the only father figure I ever had and my kids lost their Grandpa who they loved very much.

When Dean and I moved into that little cottage house, Phillip came looking for me. Not to ask all kinds of questions, but to let me know he had my back. No matter what he always did. And he talked to Dean like he'd known him forever.

He spent one night with us and the next morning when we had to leave for work he was up and walked us to the door and barely stopped talking. I told him, "we've got to go."

During the spring we took all the kids to visit him up north where he lived in Lewiston, Michigan. It was a disaster for the most part, it was the first vacation we'd taken with all the kids.

Rose and Ann were still very much very sensitive and mad at me, all emotions were very raw and we had some heated discussions while there. They really didn't care for Dean and made no bones about it. I had to defend him quite a lot in the early years. Come to think of it, for a large part of our marriage. And I had to defend my kids to him as well. Seems I'd been caught up in the middle of everyone more than I care to admit. We were there for about five days and somehow made it through and back home and nobody died. We had to take two cars, which was a good thing as it gave us a little extra space for all those contained emotions.

One summer, Phillip took a trip to Louisiana and stayed on a property that he'd purchased for a few weeks and came home very sick.

He had flu-like symptoms for a couple days and by the time they'd gotten him to the hospital he was in very bad shape and had gone into a coma.

He was diagnosed with a severe case of Pneumococcal Pneumonia. When we got word that they didn't know if he was going to live we immediately left Toledo to travel 315 miles to Petoskey, Michigan, where he was in the hospital. I went with a couple of the kids. We could only stay a few days because I needed to get back to work and they had to return to school. There was nothing we could do. Phillip was holding his own. We made the trip about two or three times. He remained like that, in and out of consciousness, for several months. When he got well enough to travel they transferred him to a hospital in Ann Arbor, Michigan, so he could be closer to us and we made that trip a few times. He finally came to settle at Heritage Village of Waterville, Ohio, a nursing facility just about 20 minutes outside of town and I thought he was on the road to recovery.

I left work one evening to go and visit him. Scottie and Angie were both there. Scottie was sneaking Phillip a puff of cigarette and I told him not too! He looked at me with these sad eyes and said "Ray, he's dying." Shrugging his shoulders like, what do you want me to do? But I didn't take it seriously. I don't know if he said that and I didn't even ask him why he would say that. Didn't think that maybe he knew something that I didn't.

I didn't stay long because I had told my boss at Jeep that I'd return by a certain time. As I was traveling back I had this sudden urge to return to the hospital, but I didn't because I said I would work a half day and so I really needed to go back to work. That night I got a phone call that Phillip had passed.

I regretted for so many years not going back that night. There was nothing more important happening that I couldn't have just gone back and said, "fuck it, my dad needs me."

Junior, Marie, and stepdad Philip

ANN

Ann kicked my ass that year she became a chronic runaway. I couldn't believe it was happening when she did it the first time. She was just 14 years old, but was hanging out with an older crowd. A few girls who were her friends had their own apartment. She had friends who I didn't even know. So I could never find her. She didn't come home until she was ready to come home.

The police reports were the hardest thing because they always asked if I'd be able to get dental records. Of course I could, but who wants to think that their child could be possibly out there dead somewhere. I was fascinated by angels during this time and had beautiful angel pictures on my walls and statues of angels and the thought of them brought me lots of comfort. That was how I spent most of my evenings while Ann was away from home – in my living room surrounded by thoughts of angels protecting my child.

I would pray to God to send all the angels he could spare to surround her and keep her safe. It was the only thing that kept me sane during that time. I'd hold vigil all night long not being able to go to sleep until dawn. I just couldn't sleep not knowing where my daughter was.

I had a very good friend who worked on dispatch for Toledo Police Department and she told me anytime I had a tip to call her and she'd send someone right out. One evening I did call her and I gave her an address that I thought Ann might be at and about 30 minutes later she called me to let me know that they had found a runaway there but it wasn't my daughter Ann.

At times I had to laugh at Ann's boldness; she did things I'd never thought of doing. I would cut the wires in her bedroom to keep her off the phone late at night and she rewired them. I had to take the phones to work with me to keep her off of them. She would smoke in her bedroom and throw her butts out the window. The neighbor told me she was the one picking them up. Even had me buying her cigarettes at 16 just to keep her happy. Hell, I could barely afford my own habit and I was smoking more than ever since I'd quit drinking. I know it was wrong to buy her cigarettes at that age, but let's just face it I was desperate to try to keep my family together. I was holding my breath and holding on by a string at times.

I had to have her arrested right out of the home and committed to Charter Hospital, a behavioral hospital for weeks at a time. She hated me for that. She spent time in juvenile hall and had to go before a judge. He took a liking to her immediately and put her on house arrest. House arrest was fine with me, aside from being disrespectful and talking back and calling me out of my name at least I knew where she was. I learned that if her mouth was moving she was lying – lying about going to school, lying about who she was with, lying about whatever to get what she wanted. The judge told her if she even thought about staying home from school she had to call him for permission.

I don't know what I would've done without the help from the Friesners, Grandma and Grandpa, and Aunt Krissy. They helped both Ann and I tremendously during this very hard transition. Robert Friesner was the man my mom was married to (you may remember from earlier in the book) whose last name I carried but said wasn't really my dad. They didn't have to do what they did for any of us but I really am appreciative.

One night while I was working on the line I was having a really hard time, thinking about everything that was going on. I felt as if the floodgates were going to open and there would be no stopping all the tears that had been bottled up. So during a break I asked to see my union steward and they sent me to a trailer outside that they were using as a temporary office. It was the first time they heard what I had going on both with my divorce and the kids. I could not stop crying as I shared what I'd been hiding for too long. I just wanted to go home. They got me right out of there! I had to call the Friesners to come and pick me up. I was unable to even drive. I was a basket case. And they told Ann that she really needed to start thinking of others and not just herself. Grandma Friesner told Ann the state I was in when she had to pick me up and it was not pretty.

Dean was so upset with me because he didn't realize what had happened. And I had to tell him that I didn't want to have a meltdown right there on the line. I knew as soon as I opened my mouth the floodgates were going to open.

Ann stayed with the Friesners for a time. Grandpa Friesner would get up and take her to school. You've got to understand this man didn't find out about me until I was 17 years old. That's when I finally met them. Robert Friesner and his wife Maryann thought that he was my father. They threw a baby shower for me when I was pregnant with Rose. Only for me to have to tell them later that he wasn't my father after all. And they still accepted me and my children as family.

At times I felt like I didn't have anyone to talk to, not even Dean. I felt as though my kids were my problem and I didn't want them to have the opportunity to tell Dean, "You're not our dad, you can't tell us what to do!" And so I didn't tell him most things that concerned the kids, I just dealt with them on my own. He handled his and I handled mine the best we could.

Dean was in the same boat as I was in. He felt alone as well, like he couldn't talk to me about certain things that he was dealing with. We were both so very frustrated at times and we would take it out on each other in different ways. At times I looked at Dean as being very needy, but really all he wanted was for me to be there for him, too, just as I'd said that I would countless times.

I just wanted to be in my own thoughts most of the time, which he thought meant giving him the silent treatment and he would have none of that! He wanted to talk everything out where we were concerned. He expressed to me that this was a new relationship and that the silent treatment may have worked in the past, but that's not how we should handle things now. He was right. He had a way of making me see that things weren't really that bad. That there was nothing we couldn't handle together. He constantly showed me through his actions that he loved me and was standing by me no matter how ugly I got or the situation.

When you've been hurt you act differently. There were times when I was afraid to speak out about things for fear of being judged. I covered for my family all my life for fear of them being judged as well as my kids.

When Rose had her first sexual encounter at 15, Lee went nuts as well as when she started menstrating. He couldn't handle it, literally.

When Ann started liking black boys I sensed some prejudice in Dean.

I had not been raised to be prejudiced but I thought I needed to protect her from those who were and so I forbade it. It made me look bad even though it was not who I was.

So I kept to myself a lot of things that were happening with the kids. If Dean asked I would share with him but most of the time he didn't ask.

Xavier, Ann, Rachel, Ray, Junior, James, and Rose

TRYING TO BE A FAMILY

Dean and I were learning each other's ways and starting to butt heads a little mainly where the kids were concerned.

We'd been raising our kids a certain way. He had his ways and I had mine and some things were different. They weren't major things. Like my kids were not allowed to eat cereal other than for breakfast where Paul was allowed to eat a bowl before he went to bed. So we just bought more boxes of cereal.

I would tell my kids we were going here or there and I felt that Dean gave Paul too many choices. If he didn't go with us he could go here or there and then the other kids would say that they didn't want to go either. Church was one of the places that was a real issue because I took my kids to church and since Dean didn't take Paul, my kids really fought me on it as well, and I stopped making them go after that point.

Dean tried to nudge Paul to be a little bit more independent like buttoning up his own shirts or getting his own plate of food because all the others were doing it but it just frustrated him and he would become angry and so it was just easier for Dean to do it.

We had to bring in an older person while we worked nights, just to keep the peace in the house while all the kids were there. I was not going to take any chances while we were battling it out in the court system. Otherwise we were getting calls at work that someone was fighting. It was a rare occasion because we learned fast. Kids needed supervision, especially the older ones.

We settled on an older woman named Sally, she'd been a former truck driver and all she had to do really was be present. She sat in a nice recliner all evening long watching TV and knitting as the kids came and went throughout the house and when it was time for them to go to bed she was free to go home.

They liked Sally and would talk to her and joke around with her of course and knew exactly why they had to have the supervision. We were very fortunate in that our jobs allowed us to be able to provide. I know lots of kids are home alone while their parents work, mostly single parents. It would've been a big fear for me, I've never left my kids alone.

We did have one incident where Paul pulled out a knife on Junior and we were not about to let that happen again.

I honestly felt bad for Paul. Early on I would hear Dean telling him that he needed to keep it down because I was nervous and couldn't handle much noise. And Paul was just a little guy he didn't understand. All he knew was he was in a house full of madness compared to what he was used to. It was the others who were a loud and rowdy bunch, not him.

It was a hard time for all of us. I wasn't mad at any of my kids. I was trying to be as sympathetic as I knew how. I was newly sober, learning how to do many things for the first time as a sober mom. I was uptight a lot of the time and the kids didn't see me as fun anymore. I have no doubt they pushed me to the limit as a way of testing me. Maybe they even wished that I'd go back to drinking again. I don't mean that in a bad way they were just kids and didn't know anything about being an alcoholic. It's not a topic that was ever discussed at the dinner table.

They were having to see a whole new Mom in a new light and I don't think they liked it. I stayed the course and stayed true to myself because I wanted to and I needed to because of them. I always felt like raising these kids was my one true job. The most important one, the one God gave me. My job at Jeep was just a way of supporting them and what a blessing that was.

Dean tried as he could, but never made much headway with them. I think they may have actually liked him a little bit. He taught us all to play, "Oh When The Saints Go Marching In" on the keyboard. He taught Ann to drive a stick shift in his truck, to this day she is the only one of the kids who can drive a manual vehicle. He took them to the pumpkin patch and carved pumpkins every year, they never did that with Lee. He took them sledding and on bike trails at the park.

There was just too much animosity and jealousy and everyone was so needy because of the circumstances and everything that we'd all been through. I was mentally and physically exhausted. This feeling didn't let up and seemed to intensify as time wore on. I prayed for strength, wisdom, patience, and the wherewithal to make the best decisions from there on in, because deep down I believed we all deserved to be happy.

Marriage To Dean Clark

My divorce was final in September, 1995, and Dean and I married 23 days later – on September 22, 1995. We got married in the home that we'd bought exactly one year after our meeting.

We had a justice of the peace come in and I wore an ivory color wedding dress with a handmade head piece Angie made for me. My childhood friend Susan McClain Good put my hair up beautifully. I carried a bouquet of pastel colored flowers with a single rose in the middle. I came down the stairs with my son Junior.

Dean was waiting for me in the dining area where we managed to fit about 15 family members. Standing there, handsome as ever wearing a white tuxedo with a single red rose bud in the lapel, I could tell he was fighting back tears. He'd been so nervous all morning. It was a very emotional time for both of us. The days leading up to this very day had been so hard. We couldn't believe that the time had finally arrived and we were getting married. It was bittersweet. The day before Ann had run away and she was nowhere to be found.

Dean's best man was his longtime friend and fellow band member Big John Brautigan; Angie was my maid of honor. She had been sick that day (diagnosed with Lupus) and we weren't sure she'd be able to make it. I'm so glad she did. We'd always stood by each other through everything. Throughout my entire life I know that she has prayed for me. It only makes sense that she would be standing next to me on this very important special day.

Afterwards we had a small reception at a dance hall with family and friends.

One of our coworkers was the DJ that night. We had a variety of Mexican foods that we had catered and Polish foods that the Friesners cooked themselves. The Friesners once again were a tremendous help in securing the hall for us. We danced and we laughed and for the first time my mom got a chance to meet Dean. Up until this time she'd never even so much as seen a photo of him.

Angie brought her shortly after the reception got underway and she and Tia Lupe danced well into the evening. We took lots of photos dancing with the smaller kids, Paul, Rachel, and Marie. Dean's mom was there as well as his brother and sister, and some nieces and nephews. It was a real family affair.

My closest cousins were there to help me celebrate – Angie, Mary and Izzy with their kids, David, Maryann, Gloria, cousin Ursula, and also cousin Paul, who later passed away too soon from complications due to alcohol abuse. My brother Scott was there as well as my closest childhood friends Dena and Kara.

Rachel and Marie

Dean and little Rachel

Dean and Rachel Clark Wedding
September 22, 1995

Dean and Rachel Clark Wedding

Clark Family

Angie, Rachel, and Marie

Deans mom Nancy Clark, niece Jackie, and Deans brother Mike Clark

Garcia Family

Rachel and Mom Rosa

Friesner Family

Year Two

We spent so much time writing love letters to each other that we filled an entire binder. We had to build each other up constantly because of what we were going through. I was his biggest advocate and he was mine. Letter after letter of all that we meant to each other and dreams of the future and nights together, living for the weekend. We had so much to look forward to. We just kept professing and bringing all things to life day by day. One day he would have doubts of my love for him and then another day I doubted him. And we had to keep reassuring each other that we were going to make it through these very difficult times, even when it seemed impossible at times.

Dean was needing me to be present for him and I was trying to be present for him, and my children, and Paul, and, well, everyone that it would leave me feeling so inadequate at times. I just couldn't measure up to everyone's standard, try as I might.

These letters were our life line. We were getting to know one another after fate had brought us together. He was so trusting of me in the very beginning and I of him, but the Devil would try to sow a seed of doubt in both of us and our ex spouses would steal our energy at every turn. We really did need to be a team. I was trying to maintain my sobriety and I was trying to be strong because I wanted to be a better person all around, not just a better wife or mother and daughter. I wanted to have a relationship with God. I wanted to be happy.

Rose got married after giving us just two months to plan her wedding, right after high school graduation. Oh yeah, that wasn't stressful. She had only known Dan for a few months but hey, who were we to stand in the way of love? Considering what she just watched her own mom doing... At that time I would have agreed to almost anything where my kids were concerned just to see them happy. We'd all been through so much I just wanted them to be happy.

Rose, who had been with me from the very beginning, deserved some happiness in her life. I felt like I owed her so much and I thought Dan was the one. As it turns out he was not and they ended their marriage.

Followed by bio dad calling to me to see if I'd be willing to take a paternity test, to establish my own paternity, you can't make this kind of stuff up. Imagine that after 36 years of denying a child now all of a sudden you want to know the truth.

Bio Dad

His name was Jim Cappelletty. He is deceased today, but back in the early spring of 1997 he got word to me through a mutual friend that he wanted to talk to me. So we had this very overdue conversation about establishing paternity once and for all. He told me that his wife was on board for us finding out because he'd heard that I was his but he didn't know for sure. And so I said that I would take the test. It wasn't for me that I agreed to but more so for my mom. Because it was something that I felt we hadn't discussed at the time but I did feel that it would be important for her to prove that he was in fact my father. And so I agreed.

On the morning that Dean drove me to Medical College Hospital for the blood test I'd been so sick with nausea. I had to lay down in the front seat for fear of just losing my cookies right then and there.

It took a very short time for the results to come back that showed I was his daughter 99.8%. Since he paid for the test he got notice the same as I did.

It wasn't long after the results came back that Jim called me to say that his wife wasn't handling the news very well and that he wouldn't be in touch with me for a while. But he wanted me to know that he'd be thinking about me.

When I gave my mom the news about the positive test she could not have been happier, she was grinning from ear to ear. But to me it made no difference. I didn't feel like I'd gained a single thing. My dad had passed already in my eyes just a few short months ago. That's what mattered to me most and I never gave it a second thought. I had way too much on my plate.

After Jim's wife passed, we were reacquainted and I went on to meet my half siblings Lori, Monti, Nick, and Rocco.

They kinda knew about me already had heard the rumors through the years but out of respect for their mother they never asked any questions. I totally get that. She lost two daughters, one was my age which means their mother was pregnant about the same time as my mother was. Another daughter was killed in a motorcycle accident, before she herself passed. That's some heartache right there, unimaginable heartache.

In one conversation with my half brother Nick he shared with me what it was like growing up with their father who was an alcoholic. He said it was not good and that I was better off most likely and I tend to agree.

Jim passed away in 2013. My half brother Monti, who I came to know a little bit, sadly passed away as well in 2019; he was only 54 years old.

LtoR: Monti Cappelletty, wife Denise, Rachel k, Nick Cappelletty, wife Dawn

Ladies Luncheon

Angie had invited me to a ladies luncheon at a new church she found and had attended a few times. I gladly said yes and she purchased tickets for the both of us to attend. It was held right in the church, which was unlike any I'd ever been in before. Coming from a Catholic Church I was used to seeing lots of stained glass and beautiful statues but there wasn't anything like that at Cornerstone Church.

It had been a Hills department store back in the day, much like a Target or KMart.

There were big round tables set up with very nice place settings and cloth dinner napkins and tablecloth. We were served a salad with rolls and butter before the main course. We had water glasses and cups for tea or coffee. It was very elegant I thought. The ladies that were seated with us looked just as surprised as us. It was their first time attending a luncheon. We introduced ourselves and chatted a little. They gave away some prizes and had a little entertainment and Angie bought me a souvenir tee shirt with the name of the conference on it. I had such a wonderful time that I was really curious about what the church service would be like so the following Sunday Dean and I attended a service.

CHURCH

We had been looking for a church to attend as a family. We'd gone to a Catholic Church once and never even made it inside because we forgot to set our clocks ahead, as in spring forward and when we arrived church was over. It was probably a good thing because the kids fussed so much that one of them, Paul, was not even planning on getting out of the car. So we just turned around and went back home.

We were currently attending a church that had a woman pastor who preached fire and brimstone. And so I'd heard things that I'd never heard before in the church like Revelations.

The Catholic Church readings were mainly from the Gospels Mathew, Mark, Luke, and John.

I was raised Catholic my whole life. It was all we knew, all my kids knew, they were baptized in the Catholic Church but I was on a mission to get closer with God and I knew I had to leave the church I'd spent all those years in.

I always knew that God was with me and I knew that I had angels surrounding me and that they watched over my kids.

I'd never read the Bible but I started reading books about faith by authors Max Lacado – *He Chose the Nails* and *In the Eye of the Storm* – and Liz Curtis Higgs *Bad Girls of the Bible* and *Really Bad Girls of the Bible* – just to name a few. These books contained stories of everyday modern life that made them relatable to me then compared them to stories in the Bible. It made it very easy for me to comprehend.

That is how I came to even start to read the Bible. The first version I read was a women's Devotional Bible New International Version with daily devotions from Godly women.

I'm not knocking anyone's church I'm just saying that I was looking for more at the time.

It just so happened to be Fathers Day when we visited Cornerstone in Maumee, Ohio, for the first time. The message of the day was that Fathers needed to cover their daughters, in other words protect them. Do not just allow them to go off with anyone. And how there were so many absent fathers and all these daughters without any protection. And it really hit home for me. I cried like a baby. That service seemed to be geared towards me but at the same time was also true for many other women in church on that day. It touched me so much and I knew I'd found my church. There was no reason to continue to look any further. On most occasions I could relate to the Pastor's message. He had a way of explaining scripture and his interpretation of scripture that made it very easy for me to follow.

I was there every Sunday afterwards. Both Dean and I were. We didn't even bother making the kids go. We left them home sleeping and afterwards we went to breakfast. And when we told them about going to breakfast we thought it might be an incentive for them to want to get up and go but it was not.

Cornerstone is a nondenominational church, a five fold ministry that was founded by Bishop Michael Pitts in 1986 along with his wife Kathie. They had an excellent children's ministry for kids of all ages. Cornerstone had many volunteers for everything from door greeters, to ushers, to people running a bookstore inside, to cleaning the bathrooms. I was very impressed. Everyone was so nice and the Pastor liked to get people out of their comfort zone by having them step out from their seat and go and shake two or three peoples hands, and tell them you're glad they made it to church that particular morning. Or just turn and shake the hand of the person next to you.

Dean hated that and he would hold onto my hand and not let go! Another thing he didn't much care for was the praise and worship music that sometimes took up to a full hour before the service would start. He started to bring his Sunday newspaper with him and sit in the car for that hour before coming in. I frowned at him for doing that, but I understood. I especially liked the music myself and didn't have a problem walking in alone.

I liked that the Pastor preached order. Because all my life I have strived for order. In the manner in which I kept my house, and simple things like just cleaning up as I went along in the kitchen. It led me later on in life to Feng Shui. But in my earlier years at Jeep sometimes they would have me sweep the floor. And I think I was probably the best sweeper they ever had. I take pride in all things that I do. I don't believe in doing things half ass, and I don't appreciate it when others do it either. I love excellence. I love doing all things unto the Lord. Even cleaning the bathroom, which is my very least favorite job to do in the whole house. I put on my headphones and blast the praise and worship music.

PREGNANCY

Dean and I found out that we were expecting twins in the year 1997. It was the nausea I was feeling in the car on that day I went in for the paternity test.

You talk about a surprise, a very wonderful surprise no doubt.

When we learned we would have two baby boys, we were overjoyed and full of anticipation for their arrival. But the pregnancy proved to be a little complicated after just four months when I was put on very strict bed rest due to placenta previa and hypertension.

Paul did not stay with us long after hearing the news of the pregnancy. I was home and not needing Sally to come to sit with the kids any longer and one night while in my room I heard this music coming from Paul's room and as I listened to it realized that there was cussing and use of the N word and just totally music that I didn't approve of and I went to his room and told him he was not allowed to listen to that kind of music and told him that he needed to turn it off right away!

Whereas he proceeded to call me all kinds of names and told me to get out of the room!

I had to call Dean home from work, because my blood pressure was getting way too high. I was livid!

Dean came home right away and gave Paul a whipping! And he told him if he couldn't respect me he would have to go and live with his mom. And Paul chose to go live with his mom that very night.

Yes of course I felt bad at the time and I still do to this day because I know that had to affect him after all the time spent with his dad alone. Over the years I've tried to convey that to Dean, but he's been in denial about it.

There have been several women in and out of Dean's life and Paul has been a little rough on a couple of us.

Since I was home alone now I would sneak out while Dean was working the second shift and go to church on Thursday evening. He didn't have a clue, I parked the van in the same spot every night just like he left it. All I wanted to do was praise the Lord. I wanted to be in the house worshiping and thanking Him for what he'd done for me.

You see, that night that I was sitting in that bar and I told the Lord that he was going to have to help me and that I couldn't do it without Him. He let me know that he was right there with me and would be there every step of the way! So I was not fearful of leaving my house to go to the house of worship. How could anything be wrong with that? I especially loved the music from the choir, dancing, clapping, and jumping up and down! Yes, jumping up and down! It was very lively and they liked people to partake in the praise and worship, it had a way of stirring things up in me. Bringing my emotions to the forefront with lots of tears and I always felt like I'd been cleansed when it was time to go.

He blessed me with two baby boys, he gave me all my kids back. I was awarded custody after the Guardian ad litem report came back advising they be returned to me shortly after the babies were born. He gave me so much insight as to how to live my life going forward. He taught me about forgiveness and about patience.

Some may read this book and say that we were lusting for each other and therefore sinning and God would not bless our union. And that may be true, but I didn't know about lust at the time. I learned about it in one of our services and it scared me. I knew I had to repent. But I also knew that God knew my heart as evident in all of our letters. We barely spoke in lustful ways. But I've determined that only God could judge me on that. Hence why I often say that I live in a glass house. You won't find me pointing the finger at anyone when three others are pointing right back at me.

I also felt as though I was damned to hell not only because I left the husband of my youth, but I was instrumental in breaking up Dean's marriage as well.

I told myself that his marriage was one big mistake and had he held out and waited on me it never would've happened. Some people just cannot bear the thought of being alone, I am Dean's forth wife.

Early on as I was learning the Christian way, whenever Dean thought that I'd done something or I was acting in such a way that may not have been very Christian like, he would tell me that he didn't think the Pastor would approve. And to that I would get very defensive because I felt like he was judging me where he had no right. I was and am after all still human and will always be growing and moving forward in my Christian walk.

As a way of repenting for my sins and seeking forgiveness from God I decided to be baptized in water. It was an outward expression of an inward change that I was happy to do, I was realizing my faults and it hurt to see myself in that manner.

I took First Principal classes for eight weeks and was then baptized by the Holy Spirit. It is a sacrament through which a believer, through the laying on of hands and the prayer of an apostle, receives the gift of the Holy Spirit. In some cases you will begin to speak in tongues and or fall out but I did neither. Though I have done both at other times.

I absolutely feel led by the Holy Spirit every day, He makes me want to be more Christ-like. He renews my mind and convicts me of sin and leads me to repentance.

The Holy Spirit impressed upon me one day that God was not looking down on my mom thinking, "that Rosa was a real bitch!" And I shouldn't be thinking that either!

If I wanted to be forgiven for the things I'd done then I need to forgive as well.

I'd been holding back on my mom – love, understanding, patience, empathy, all these things I refused to show her because I was holding a grudge for the times she'd left us alone. The times there was no food or when the gas, water, or electricity got cut off.

I had purchased a pink Woman of Faith Hat at one of the ladies conferences and I would wear it whenever I went to see my mom. If I was dreading having to go, Dean would tell me to go put my hat on and go. It acted as a reminder to me to treat others, including my mom, with kindness. I became a different person with that hat on.

Another reason that I vowed never to touch alcohol again is I believe that God will not be mocked. He took the want for alcohol completely away from me as though that part of my life never even existed. He may not do it again.

TWINS

Bedrest alone was not working well. Even though I got up only to use the bathroom and shower as quickly as I could, I continued to have high blood pressure. I would monitor in bed just laying there and it would be high. Every one of my doctor appointments landed me in the hospital for at least an overnight.

The week of Christmas 1997 I was in the hospital, desperate to be able to be at home for Christmas to be with the kids. I had to beg my doctor, Dr. Ann Smith, to discharge me and she relented on the condition that the following morning I would check myself back in for the duration. Meaning until the babies were born.

We had a wonderful Christmas, I'm sure it was way more stimulating than what Dr. Smith would have approved of, with all the excitement, but we made it through and I held true to my word.

Dean had been given lists periodically to go and make purchases for me of gifts to give the kids for Christmas and I was very appreciative of that. Rose had done some shopping for me and Angie as well. It was all hands on deck to make it as special as we could given the circumstances.

I returned to the hospital without delay and began my stay.

New Year's Eve came and I was allowed visitors for a very short while. Too much excitement.

I would bury my head in my pillow to stifle the laughter while watching Lucy, because if the nurses caught me they would turn my TV off. They didn't want me having any type of emotional expression because it would raise my blood pressure, the situation was that volatile.

The nurses caring for me were amazing, bringing me the *Blade Daily* (a Toledo Newspaper), painting my fingernails, and feeding me late night snacks of turkey sandwiches and peanut butter crackers. (smile)

We knew that the babies were going to come early, we just didn't know how early. I took some steroid shots to improve their lung function.

They were due to arrive early March and instead came on January 12, 1998.

They said baby #2 was kicking baby #1 and causing stress, his heart rate was beginning to drop and an emergency C-section was in order. They were born two months early. Baby #1, James, weighed in at 2 pounds, 10 ounces. Baby #2, Ray, weighed slightly more, at 3 pounds.

Both babies were born amazingly without any issues aside from the birth weight. They came out breathing on their own. James had to be fed through a tube for a short while but due to their size they spent 30 days in the NICU to gain some weight before we were allowed to bring our little bundles of joy, our miracle babies, home.

Although I had a C-section, we visited them every single day before Dean went to work. One day we arrived to find one of the isolettes empty and panicked immediately.

Come to find out they had put the brothers together in one, just like they were used to being since conception.

After 30 days, that's when the fun started. Dean and I went to opposite shifts so that we could raise our kids. It's all a blur today, many sleepless nights and I'm not sure how we did it, I just know that we did. By the grace of God and the help of all the older kids. The boys were loved by all and there were plenty of helping hands. The rest is history, as they say.

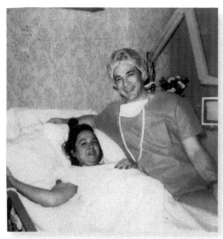

Twins are born, delivery day January 12, 1998

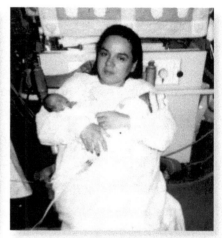

Rachel with newborn twins James and Ray

Angie holding Ray, Ann holding James

Junior with James and Ray

Ray and James

Prom - L-R Marie, Ray, James, and Rachel

L - R Ray, Dean, and James Clark

James, Ray, Paul Clark

George Clark (Dean's dad) and look-a-like Ray

Ray and James Clark

Dean Loses His Parents

I was on bed rest at home when Dean lost his mother. It was a very difficult time for him yet he needed to remain strong. He was working and taking care of me as well as all the kids when they were there as his mom was dying.

She had had a stroke and was in rehabilitation when they put a pacemaker in thinking that would help her and she eventually started going downhill. Dean believed she was just tired and had lost her will to live.

So this particular evening while visiting with her she was coherent enough that he was able to tell her that he loved her and he'd thought she was the best mom ever. She acknowledged him and he could see a tear forming in the corner of her eye and when he left believed it to be just a matter of time and she would pass.

Shortly after arriving back home he received the phone call that she had indeed passed. I was about four months pregnant with the twins when we laid her to rest.

I spent only a very short time with her, but it was evident that Dean and his mom shared a very special bond. He had told me once that he was the only baby she was able to stay at home with to raise.

The twins spent 30 days in the NICU after they were born due to their size and weight. Dean's father, George Clark, never got a chance to lay eyes on them other than in a photo Dean had taken for him to see, as he unexpectedly passed away. Dean had been to see him the night before he passed. Dean told him that he'd return the next day with a television set for his room, in which George replied "what for."

God was the one who got us through during that time. Whether you're a believer or not or you just want to take all the credit yourself I'm not trying to convince anyone of anything. I'm just telling you what I believe to be true for us.

Dean's parents George and Nancy Clark

Rosa Garcia and James

Dear friend and prayer warrior
Jackie Barnes and Rachel Clark

Mom Passes

I didn't see my mom very much during the time I was going through the divorce and custody. I didn't want to worry her and I definitely didn't want to have to explain everything that was happening. I had too much going on and my circle was very small and tight. But after things calmed down and she finally got a chance to meet Dean (at the wedding) it was back to things as usual.

Up until that time Scott was also maintaining sobriety, he was sober and taking care of Mom the best way he could. He walked everywhere and then bought a bike which made traveling for everyday things like cigarettes and pop much easier. She loved Chinese food from the New China King down on Broadway, or Taco Bell.

He always got her whatever she wanted. Scott remains sober today. I celebrate his accomplishments because for a while it was very bad. I feared for his life. He wasn't making good decisions.

As a young woman my mom was put on Valium. She told me that it was after having had some kind of seizure that she believed to be epilepsy. She remained on them for many years. It's amazing to me to this day that she remained on them for so long after having had just one seizure, and when she quit drinking at the age of 36 she added a few other pills. She simply put one crutch down and picked up another. Darvocet was prescribed after she was diagnosed with thoracic outlet syndrome as well as Tylenol 3s that she would buy from her friend Velma.

She was constantly asking me for money to buy what she referred to as her medicine. I told her that all of her medicines were covered by her insurance and anything she had to purchase from her friends were considered drugs to me and I wasn't going to pay for them. I refused and so she would kick me out of her house and tell me not to come back.

She knew that Dean took prescription meds for a back injury and wanted me to get her some from him but I wasn't about to start that. I knew first hand how she was abusing the pills, taking them like candy, she was always running out. Once she claimed to accidentally drop them down the sink while trying to take one.

She was diagnosed with uterine cancer and at the time I was working the first shift and as a means to help her I put in for a transfer to go to the second shift so that I could take her for daily treatments.

The uterine cancer had metastasized to her hip and required low radiation treatments every day for nine weeks with only the weekend off. I was the only one who could take her, since neither my brother Scott nor my mom drove. I needed to be free during the day.

I would leave my house at 1 PM to drive across town to pick her up, take her to the Medical College of Ohio Hospital for treatment then back home. And then I went to work for 10 hours. Dean was home with the boys in the evening after school and we both did what we needed to do.

Honestly I didn't know how she was going to beat cancer, I didn't think she was strong enough. She seemed very frail to me at just 85 pounds and I was very scared.

174

The day before we found out that she had cancer I visited her with full intention of leading her to salvation, because I didn't know where she stood, what her beliefs were. She had not attended church in many years and being in the Catholic church there are rituals like praying the rosary and praying to Mary and the Saints who Catholics believe pray to God on our behalf.

In my newly formed relationship with God I learned to pray and speak directly to him, there was no need to go through the saints. And so I asked my mom if she wanted to accept Jesus into her life and pray the sinner's prayer with me?

We never discussed my church or my pastor but on this day she told me that she wanted to believe in my God she seemed scared in some way and I had to reassure her that it was the same God as hers that there was only one God and it was the same one as in the Bible, did she want to accept his Son Jesus into her heart? She said yes, she did.

According to Wikipedia, "The Sinner's Prayer is an Evangelical Christian term referring to any prayer of repentance, prayed by individuals who feel convinced of the presence of sin in their lives and have the desire to form or renew a personal relationship with God through Jesus Christ."

I'm so happy to be able to say that she did beat cancer. She was ready every day with a bottle of water and sometimes I'd get her a wheelchair if she expressed that she was feeling tired. I had gotten very close to her during this time and I wanted to be there for her. I knew she was being strong.

Then one day I arrived to pick her up and she was to see the doctor on this visit and she and my brother Scott were stoned as hell. She was falling asleep in the wheelchair and he was falling asleep standing up against a wall. I was so pissed! Yelling at both of them on the drive home I'm sure they never even remembered, the doctors and the nurses never said anything about it. I delivered them back home and I went on to work.

I was shocked one day on another visit when they brought her out from her radiation treatment and she told me that they had checked her for lice. I couldn't believe it. She said they had found a bug on the bed and thought it was from her.

But when they checked and found she didn't have lice they just shrugged it off never mentioning it to me at all. I was very upset, I didn't say anything because I didn't want to bring any more embarrassment to her. It really hurt my feelings. But my mom acted like it was no big deal. She had told me stories of getting lice as a little girl and she would pull the bug out herself and listen to it crack between her nails as she smashed them. That's how she killed them. (laughing) You can't make this stuff up!

One night while I was still working, Scott called me to tell me that Mom was acting funny.

He said they were watching TV and she started talking incoherently making conversation that didn't make any sense. And he was worried. So I took a ride to their house after I got off work to see for myself and by the time I got there she was fine. So I didn't really know if it was her or if it was him taking too many of the pills. We just kinda sat there looking at each other, my brother and I, for a little while and then I left.

Since I refused to give her money for the pills she wanted to buy from her friends she just started using her own money. Then she wouldn't have any for food or for her favorite Pepsi or cigarettes and so I had to take her groceries or I would feel guilty. I took her care packages or if I made dinner I would take her a couple plates of food for her and my brother Scott.

By taking these pills she masked anything that she had going on and wouldn't keep doctors appointments because they wouldn't give her what she wanted.

I would visit and she'd be wearing two pairs of readers that Scott probably bought at Rite Aid because she couldn't see the TV. I offered to take her to get glasses, she had gone many years before that but would not go again.

In the end she passed because she had a blockage to her lower bowel and it began to die. Gangrene set in and by the time they caught it it was too late. She was taken by ambulance in the middle of the night and they performed an emergency surgery to remove all that was infected, this included the bowel. She would've had to have a colostomy, but following the surgery she never regained consciousness. I thought they had given her something for pain and that was why she was asleep but it was not the case. I asked the nurse who was attending to her about this. She told me they were not keeping her sedated and that she had not woken up yet. I started to ask another question because I wanted to be clear, I had just returned from a quick trip home to get the boys off to school and I was trying to find out exactly what was happening. But she interrupted me this time and said, "you know your mother is not going to live, don't you?" With that, I lost it. I broke down standing right there beside her bed at that moment it just didn't seem real. The very next thing I heard was the nurse telling me that she was going now as she showed me that her heart rate was dropping. Ever so slowly it was dropping and I leaned in real close and spoke my last words to my mom. I was heartbroken and not ready for this in any way, shape, or form. Afterwards I went one by one giving each of the kids present, Rose, Ann, Marie, Junior who had driven all night from Tennessee, and cousin Izzy, a hug, they were as heartbroken as I was. As more family arrived and we gathered ourselves and consoled each other it became real.

In the beginning when she was fairly healthy she would make up ailments trying to get prescription drugs. They gave her what they felt she needed but she wanted more. Then when things really started to go wrong they wouldn't believe her. You could say she cried wolf but I do believe that they weren't looking for the right things. At one point she'd spent a week in the hospital running this and that test, never gave her anything to eat for days and never found anything. She complained that she had no energy. But they never checked her heart. I feel like the doctors let her down here. At one point I was prepared to hire an attorney to file a malpractice suit but I was advised against it given that it was a government run hospital. The attorney said that there was no way I could win a case against them.

Mom passed when the twins, James and Ray, were 10 years old, leaving them with no grandparents.

Just like that she was gone.

I had seen her a few days before. On my way to work I stopped to drop her groceries and she'd been laying on the sofa. For days she was complaining of not having any energy. I'd taken her to the doctor's office and they prescribed Ensure drinks for her, to give her body the nutrients it needed for strength and energy.

As usual I was in a hurry, running late, and I just dropped the groceries off in the kitchen for Scott to take care of and as I was leaving she had her arms outstretched to me. Thanking me and telling me that she didn't know what she would've done without me and that she loved me so much. To which I mumbled, "Yeah, yeah, I know." And off I went never to see her alive again.

After she passed, that vision of her laying on that sofa with her arms outstretched tormented me. I couldn't put it out of my mind.

Why was I always having to be in a hurry? Why was that damned job so important? I had FMLA (Family Medical Leave) for her and her condition specifically. I could take care of her no questions asked where it involved my employment if I was late arriving or needed to take a day off.

Guilt will eat you alive if you let it.

I had this friend Jackie who was a real prayer warrior and we worked on the same team at Jeep putting doors on. And one day I was telling her about the vision I had of my mom just before her death and how it was making me so sad just seeing it over and over in my mind and she got me in the break room and laid hands on me and prayed over me right away. She explained to me that it was the Devil that was trying to torment me and I believed it.

Afterwards I tried as I might, but I couldn't see the vision anymore. It's like it was behind a veil. Once I was trying really hard and it was right there so close I had to stop myself.

I once had prayed for the Lord to just take her, I told her what a miserable life it must be to have to be worried about where your next pill is coming from. I know how harsh it sounds. I don't think at the time I realized the finality of it. And so the guilt set in for everything I ever said that was disrespectful and dishonorable to my mother. The woman who carried me and gave me life was far from perfect but still she didn't deserve the angry words I had for her.

I wished I'd been more understanding while she was alive.

For Mother's Day she loved to have me read the cards out loud to her and I took great pains in doing so. WHY? It was a simple gesture. In the store I would pick up the cards and begin to read and if it said something like you taught me all these things or any kind of accolades that I didn't feel fit the profile, I would put that card back. I was not buying anything too mushy or giving credit I felt she didn't deserve. Gosh how stupid I feel to have to be admitting this! It's the Holy Spirit wanting me to come forward as a way of letting things go once and for all. It just doesn't do any good to beat myself up anymore. What's done is done and I could not be more sorry.

The kids and I never laughed so hard as we did once when we went to pick her up to bring her to dinner. I pulled up in an alley that was right next to her house, and tooted my horn to let her know I had arrived. She waved to me from the window and as we watched her come out the front door along with her was her little dog (mutt of some kind) named Mindy. She never let Mindy out if you can imagine, and Mindy was trying to make a mad run for it.

She reached out and grabbed that poor dog by the butt, and then lost her balance and went down herself. This is playing out before our eyes in what seemed to be slow motion and we were just sitting in the van kinda in shock. Then we all burst out laughing at the scene while she starts yelling for help. I yell at the kids to go and help her all the while laughing! There was non-stop laughter the entire way back home, but you really had to be there to appreciate this comedy scene and see the look on Mom's face.

I never went to her house and she didn't put something in my hand as I was leaving. A pack of cigarettes, or a 20 dollar bill, once it was a pair of earrings! Something always.

She was funny and everyone who met her loved her and the world was a better place when she was still in it.

My Mom was not perfect; she did the very best she knew how to at the time. I just wish I'd had that realization early on. And not wasted so much time feeling let down.

I'd had a dream right after Tia Lupe died that she had come back from the dead!

I asked her, "What are you doing?"

Tia Lupe replied, "I came back."

My mom was with her in the dream and I asked my Mom, "What are you doing?" And she said, "I came back too."

At the time she wasn't even dead! But now she is, now she really is. I will surely rejoice when I get to see her again. I know she'll embrace me and I will be like her little child again.

Mom, Tia Esperanza, and Tia Lupe. Sister Esperanza's only visit to the United States

Here is something I shared with my mom:

1 Peter 3:15

But in your hearts revere Christ as Lord.

Always be prepared to give an answer to everyone who asks you to give the reason for the hope that you have. But do this with gentleness and respect.

We are all on this Earth to share the word of God, to glorify Him in every way every day! To bring the message of His son Jesus Christ and salvation through the belief.

I am always going to give praise no matter what, because I know what he has brought me through. Even the prayers that went unanswered were for my good.

God's will be done, it's not always about what we want.

I stand in the gap for those who can't pray for themselves like my grandson who suffers from Mental Illness and the unborn child.

Steps To Salvation

1. Trust Jesus Christ today!...

2. Admit that you are a sinner and that you need God's help...

3. Be willing to change your mind and turn from your sin (repent)...

4. Believe that Jesus Christ died for you, was buried, and rose from the dead...

5. Through prayer, invite Jesus into your heart to become your personal Lord and Savior...

6. Pray...

Rachel Clark, brother Scott, and mom Rosa Garcia

Lesson 4
Look to Help Others Win

My mom was not a tough person to love, some of the things she did or things she would say clouded that knowledge for me. Anger wouldn't allow me to look past it but it wasn't who she was but the behavior.

I only wish I knew back then what I know now. I wish I could have shown just one more ounce of compassion while she lived still. I tortcherd myself with feelings of guilt after her passing And I know of others who are going through the same thing currently.

A very close family member said to me recently about his mom, "I am as nice to her as I can possibly be, given the circumstances." That hurt me so much to know that that was me as well at one time.

If you can remember that a is the greatest gift of all and it's free to give and you can give it anytime and everyone deserves it, you will have no regrets later to look back on.

Hold that hand, buy that special card that means

and says so much. Give a compliment. Apologize, have those hard talks to clear the air and answer questions honestly.

Spend time with family when they invite you, go! Invite them! Family is everything and sometimes you gotta love them right where they're at.

Say yes more or say no more whatever the case may be. Don't allow anyone to just use you. I'm not trying to imply that at all just use your better judgment.

I like to think that some of my actions have rubbed off on my own children.

They are some of the most considerate, compassionate, loving kids I've ever known and No I'm not just saying that because they are mine. They are forgiving towards others and when push comes to shove and it has been there for each other and for me.

Because when one wins, we all win.

If all else fails, Buy A Pink Hat.

Fast Forward Dreams

I never remembered dreaming before sobriety. I read somewhere that we dream every night, but sometimes we just don't remember. I started remembering my dreams, though some were scary dreams, like when Ama came back from the dead, and I was so happy to see her. She was sweeping with a broom right in the house where she lived before passing and I was trying to tell her how happy I was to see her, but she kept turning her back to me. I was crying and I just wanted to see her face. Then I caught a glimpse of her from the side, her profile, and she was snarling like a demon and I knew right away that it wasn't her and I had to be the one to tell everybody.

It took a long time for me to be able to tell that dream to anyone without crying. I was very close to my Ama even though I was only 20 when she passed.

In other dreams I would be at work and be in the hole.

For those that don't know what that means I can explain.

On the assembly line at Jeep you have an area in which to work in. They usually run about eight to ten feet in length depending on the job and if you don't complete your job in that area you're considered to be in the hole.

Now mind you, you're working with air tools that are suspended from the overtop of you and connected to lines overhead. You're carrying various parts of the car to install, maybe a mallet in hand or any other kind of tool required to build a vehicle and things can get hairy! Just one wrong move or if you happen to drop a part it's very easy to get in the hole. I've been on jobs where I couldn't even take time out to tie my shoes.

Who can forget Lucy in the Chocolate Factory? What a hysterical scene that was! And if you haven't ever seen it, suggest you do so on Youtube. It's classic.

So many nights in my dreams I've been able to relate to this and I wake up now thanking God that those days are over.

But not just in my dreams in real life I had an incident while on the line.

I was walking backwards, sometimes it becomes necessary as the line moves and you have to move with it. I tripped over my hoses and fell down to the ground. My partner who was working next to me ran over to me, he was a big guy, his name was Joe. Tall is what I mean. He was standing over top of me looking a little shocked and asked me if I was alright?

To which I replied all the while laughing "Do I look alright?"

He reached out his hand to help me out of the tangled mess! Workers up and down the line were watching us, I was perfectly fine. The only thing that hurt was my ego, just a little bit.

After my neighbor was shot in his own apartment, I dreamt that I was shot in the head and lay dying in front of my kids

I've dreamt that I've driven my car off a cliff.

I've even dreamt that I was in the military and that I'd overslept and the Drill Sergeant was looking for me and I was trying to hide. Once I had to stand in formation with my duffle on the top of my head! These came to me right after the twins James and Ray went to basic training. So go figure.

Fast Forward To What I Know

The one thing that I know for a fact today is had I not stopped drinking I would not be alive to tell my story 27 years later.

Marriage is hard work that is no lie. Divorce is hard on all involved. Blending families is hard work, quitting drinking, all hard work.

There was a time when I listened to the popular relationship radio talk show host, Dr. Laura, on the radio every day on my drive home. If I had taken her advice, I would have stayed in the marriage for as long as we were raising the children. Thank God I chose to follow my heart instead.

In doing so I've also spent many years seeking forgiveness from my children and myself, but most importantly from God.

I've spent many years trying to fix things that I felt were wrong because of the choices I made.

Ann running away from home, and then a teen pregnancy. She gave me my first grandchild, Xavier, who is 23 years old and the reason I'm called Granny to this day.

Promiscuity with all three of the girls.

Junior anger issues.

Paul and his relationship with his dad.

All these things I attributed to my own selfishness and wanting to be happy with Dean at any cost. And it has weighed very heavily on my heart.

Our relationship has been very strained at times

throughout the years. We've both done and said things that have hurt the other. Things that can never be taken back.

We are human, though, and we do make mistakes and fall short of the grace of God but he forgives us before we even forgive ourselves and he loves us in spite of it all.

I can't convey how many times I've sat at the dinner table next to Dean and thought about one thing or another that he's done to make me feel hurt or angry, causing me to make a snarky remark or criticize something he did or didn't do that wasn't to my liking. Only to feel convicted later on. Because God will do that to you. He has put the Holy Spirit in us and once you know you cannot pretend to not know.

And so the Holy Spirit will nudge me and put me back in my place. He softens my heart gently and I'm reminded of how it was in the beginning.

That and also the twins James and Ray would never allow me to be critical of their dad. They were ready to defend him in an instant and he came out looking like a rose and I a thorn. I often accused Dean of being overly sensitive because if I tried to make any suggestion he would respond that I was just never happy. Yes I was being critical but not for no reason.

Telling him to change out the dish rag daily made total sense to me.

It was useless and oftentimes resulted in my sitting and eating dinner in silence.

I give God all of the glory for where I am today, I put one foot in front of the other and every day I strive to be Christ-like. Some days are harder than others. I'm not gonna lie. But I have forgiven myself and I know that I am yet worthy of love. Others are not responsible for how I feel, try as I may to blame others for my feelings, I alone have to process the things that have happened in my life. And you have to do the same.

It makes me sad that Dean doesn't think that I love him sometimes because that couldn't be further from the truth. I do love him but it just seems to me that we have grown apart in some ways – we don't have fun together like we used to, we don't laugh together like we used to we just don't enjoy the same things and we go through some of our days just kind of mundane and love has nothing to do with it because I do love him with all my heart. It's kind of hard to explain. I'm still trying to figure it out myself.

For so many years we had so many distractions in our lives and for 15 years we actually worked opposite shifts so we could raise the twins.

Dean then retired and I continued to work three more years. In the last five years the twins have gone into the military and each has married. James and his wife Sophia have a baby named Cassius. He's the sweetest baby boy with bright blue eyes, the first grandchild for us to have blue eyes.

Ray is married to Jasmine.

Dean and I are working on getting reacquainted again. It's like two people finding each other all over again. If we want this marriage to continue it's gonna take more hard work.

Communication is the key. I learned that when I broke my ankle a few years back.

I was mad after a few days when I felt like Dean wasn't taking care of me the way I thought he should.

Then I realized that men and women just don't think alike, they are different kinds of caretakers. I wanted Dean to read my mind I guess and to know what I needed in advance, but all I had to do really was tell him what I wanted or needed. He was willing to do whatever I asked for.

I have three grown children at various stages of alcoholism today like myself.

Some use alcohol as a way to cope while others may have inherited a gene that makes them have a more addictive personality. I cannot speak on the science of it all. I just know that when my mom quit drinking and then became addicted to pain pills, it became a great fear of mine that I would follow in her footsteps. And so I went to great lengths to stay away from certain medication that I knew could become addictive. I believe that made me supportive as a parent can possibly be because I've been in their shoes.

I couldn't be more proud of the adults my children have become given the environment they grew up in.

Four of Dean's and my children have and continue to serve our country in the military.

Little Rachel went to the Army right out of high school and has one daughter Tianna.

Paul deployed to Iraq right in the middle of a war and is newly married to Stephanie.

Ray served in the Army for five years, deployed to the southern border and became a sergeant in his infantry unit of Rakkasans.

James currently serves in the Ohio National Guard, for almost six years now and is going to deploy in September 2022.

Rose and husband Tom will be celebrating 15 years of marriage and have one daughter Sydney.

Ann is married to Henry and she has five children: Xavier, Shakor, Anahelese, Cambria, and Odessa.

Junior currently lives with his son Ezekeil in Tennessee.

Marie is currently unmarried and has no children residing in Tennessee.

All are loving, supportive individuals, they hold jobs, and are great parents. Who could ask for more?

But life is a struggle, it gets harder out here every day. You have to learn how to maneuver through it.

I want to be able to fix things as any mother would. But it's out of my control and in the very hands of God. He is more than capable, you just have to trust Him. As long as you're alive there is always hope I believe. You just have to keep the Faith.

A very good friend of mine once said, "I'm sick if I drink, and I'm sick if I don't drink, so I may as well drink."

I don't see it that way. Because I wanted to live and I chose to live! Not just for myself, yes of course that was the first thing, but for my kids and my family. The whole family is in pain when one person hurts. I was a part of a big family who loved me and who I loved and I wanted to live for them. I wanted to raise my children to give them a good life and to protect them as a mother should.

I wasn't always able to do what I only wish but I have always prayed for a hedge of protection around them and have trusted in God to do what I couldn't.

We have certainly had our struggles as a family.

Junior didn't talk to me for three years because he got offended by something I said about his wife.

During that time he became very close to his mother-in-law. She was there for him when he was diagnosed with high blood pressure and placed on medication. She called him and was able to fill my role as mom. And it took a long time for him to even call me Mom again. But I tried to be as understanding as I could and just give him the space he needed. And I prayed we could get through this because it was so hard for me to believe that he was treating me this way over a comment that I believe I had made on social media and I was looking out for his interest, or so I thought. I thought it must be something more but if he wouldn't even engage me in conversation how would I know how to help him. It was a hard lesson for me and one that I would never make again. My kids' marriages are their own. And from now on all I do is listen. My relationship with Junior was hanging by a thread.

I was sorry for everything! I would've apologized for making him wait to be picked up from work because I was at home watching the Gaithers on TV if I had to!

Paul refuses to talk to Dean now because of things from his past. When Paul went to the Army I was able to rebuild somewhat of a relationship with him. I wrote him a letter while he was away, I explained that I was an alcoholic and during that time when he was very little I was trying to sober up. And all those times when his dad was telling him that he needed to be quiet because I was nervous, I actually was just trying to gain some peace and strength one day at a time. And I told him I was very sorry about the things he'd gone through and having to go live with his mom. I never wanted him to think that we didn't love him and that he didn't matter.

I've had one child tell me that I got what I deserved, out of anger of course or hurt feeling, what have you. But as I've said before, we are human and if God can forgive us why does anyone else think that they have the right to judge us?

Everyone has to find a way to deal with their issues. And I'll support anyone in their efforts. Because that is what family does. We support each other in healthy, positive ways.

There's no time for negativity. Life is short and fleeting. And you only get one! Imagine that, you don't get a do over.

We reassure our children when they make mistakes and that they can learn from them. Can we not as parents be given the same grace? Just as God gives us and God gives to them?

Primas L -R Ursula, Mary Ann, Alejandra, Rachel, and Gloria

Rachel and Angie

194

Family First

Rose and husband Tom Bonnette
with daughter Sydney

Ann and husband Henry Schofield

Grandkids L-R Shakor, Cambria, Ann holding Odessa, Anahelese, and Xavier

Junoir, Rachel, and grandson Ezekiel

Marie

Junior's daughter Layla

Little Rachel and Tianna

L-R Jasmine, Ray, granddaughter Sydney, Sophia, and James

James, wife Sophia, and Baby Cassius

Ray and wife Jasmine

Healing

The lord healed me from the addiction to alcohol. He took the want right away. I've never wanted another drink, it wasn't anything I've thought of even remotely since that night in the bar. It wasn't a daily struggle for me as I know that it is for a lot of people.

But not all drinkers are alcoholics. Some are heavy drinkers when given a sufficient reason to quit (work, relationships, medical reasons) can quit on their own will power and stay quit. But if they are alcoholic and alcohol has become their coping mechanism to life they will have a lot of sideways behavior while sober. Also, if the initial reason for quitting as stated earlier is lost then they will likely turn back to alcohol to fill that void.

I worked with a guy at Jeep who had to attend two AA meetings before coming to work.

It's never been like that for me.

I never had to worry about being triggered, through losses and hardships. I've kept the faith.

Through illness and accidents. I have kept the faith.

12 step programs are not for everyone, it wasn't for me. I went to a couple of AA meetings because I felt like it was the right thing to do. But I couldn't relate to some of the others that talked about losing their families or their jobs because their rock bottoms were not like mine. I determined that I needed to quit drinking. I was willing to admit that I had a problem and once I did that there was no going back. Nobody was responsible for my quitting

except for me. Nobody could have convinced me to take a drink. And you have to have that mentality in order to be able to quit. You've got to want it badly, the will to live is strong!

If you're a single parent it may not be easy to go to rehab or detox. But you can go to a hospital or urgent care to get started.

You can reach out to a family member and make getting sober a family affair. Chances are your family would be very happy to assist in any way that they could. If you know that there is a problem, believe me they do too.

You cannot be in denial of your drinking. I've never understood that concept. Most people don't stay drunk 24/7. There are some conscious moments and it's during that time of woke, realization that you know that there is a problem. But you feel like you can't or won't do anything to change it.

From day one since I've had my last drink it's as though that part of my life never even existed. I know that God will not be mocked and if I were to ever take a drink again he might not help me the next time. And I never wanted for my children or Dean to see me with a drink in my hand ever again.

I've heard too many stories of things I've done while drinking that I never want to do again.

Today most of my friends are not aware that I'm an alcoholic. Simply because I have been sober for so many years now. It's a part of my life that I don't really talk about in casual conversation.

Today I have other things to think about and stay on top of. Like my health issues.

Dean and I both had acupuncture to quit smoking. When we met he was a non-smoker who had had acupuncture once. But with everything going on he started smoking again. And he smoked two packs of cigarettes a day.

So on Valentine's Day in 2002 it was a gift for both of us to have the acupuncture.

After having quit for one year I continued with this cough I'd read was a smokers cough. But it never went away and I was diagnosed with asthma. I was foolish to think I could smoke all those years, 26, and it wouldn't do some kind of damage to my lungs.

I've had high blood pressure since turning twenty and gave birth to Ann.

I currently take medication for Diabetes. Caused by very poor eating habits all my life.

Lastly, I have carotid artery disease.

Numbness and tingling around my mouth that went ignored for many years followed by a TIA (Transient Schemic Attack) also known as a mild stroke. Diagnosed in 2017. I had surgery to open the artery but it was too late. It was already closed 98% by the time it was discovered. Also from years of smoking according to my doctor.

And so most days I'm just taking meds and trying to stay alive for as long as I can so that I may now watch my grandchildren grow.

Dean and I have been blessed with eleven grandchildren. Most are in the south with their parents but we have two who are close by. Sydney Ann Marie is 14 and a sweet little baby boy Cassius Kaine who is four months old as I write this.

Somebody once told me that there is a country song where they sing about drinking and trying to kill themselves, not literally, for the first part of their lives and trying to stay alive for the second part. I don't know if such a song is actually out there, but if I heard it, I would say, "that would be me."

A couple of times as I've laid in bed and begun to cry silently on my pillow thinking about being an alcoholic. And why did I have to be one and why was I crying? So I asked God why?

And his answer was, I cry because although I am an alcoholic, I've had some pretty amazing years.

There is no one in this world like your mother.

Honoring the memory of Prima Diane Ramirez 1962 - 2020
with daughters Jackie Rodriguez (l) and Sherae Rodriguez (r)

Honoring the memory of Christina Maddaluno
1967 - 2018
with baby Sophia Clark

201

JANUARY 12, 2022

So today the boys turn 24 years old. It's so hard to believe how fast the time goes. I heard today on the Dr. Phil show that life expectancy for women is 85 years. Well that's all well and good but I'm 60 now and I can only imagine those next 25 years will go as fast as these last 60 have! And with the kids, five of whom live out of state, we get to see them once a year. That means we'll get to see them 25 more times. I heard that somewhere as well. I don't like it much myself but what can you do when your kids move away? Nothing, either you go to them or they come home to visit. It's tough when they've got jobs and kids in school and we've got this virus to think about, but hopefully things will get better and we'll be able to spend more time together.

My Toolbox

Throughout my journey I've learned just how important it is to have a toolbox in times of crisis.

In my toolbox there is Church, my pastor with his weekly messages, and oftentimes a Thursday service as well. Well because it was just that kind of week.

There is prayer, and I mean I talk directly to God himself.

There is fellowship. (I happened to come to work in an area at Jeep where I met Denise Jackson who attended the same church that I did.)

In my toolbox is my Bible, it's a requirement if you're trying to live a Christian life.

There is also and this is way up there on the list, praise and worship music.

I blast that stuff in my ears every time I have to clean the bathroom! In the car, while I work in the yard. Anytime there is a moment of solitude is a good time for me to thank God for all that he has brought me through.

And as a military mom two times, I have a separate toolbox for the times when the news is too overwhelming with stories of conflicts and or war around the country. These days my children have crises of their own and I'm needing to keep them in prayer. It's the most important thing that I can do since most are away from home.

I tell myself that as a mom I've been given the most important job of all time.

God has entrusted me with their lives. It may not have started out on the right foot but come hell or high water, I was going to do my absolute best to not only complete the task but to improve upon it. Leave it better so that when I'm having to answer to Him at least He will know that I never quit trying. That includes not saying No, I don't tell my kids "No," at least not if I can help it.

I did not set out to write a religious book, regardless of how you interpret it. I am not a particularly religious person. I am just a woman, mother, wife, who happens to believe in a higher power and that for me is God. I don't know where I would be today had it not been for that belief. It was crucial for me.

Before he formed me in the womb and to this day at 60 years old, He has known my needs and he has watched over me and mine and has been faithful. Faithful to deliver, to heal, to set free, and bless. There is no way I could ever take credit for that which has been given to me in abundance.

I was a high school dropout, pregnant teenager, then turned to alcohol, and He made a way for me not just to live to endure, but to LIVE, to raise a family and be present for them.

When my children were in crisis, my toolbox consisted first of MONEY! (laughing) followed by prayer. It's only money and I speak of the days that I was working and earning a sizable paycheck every week. These days it's considerably smaller and it only comes once a month. It is now them sending me money, just because (as Marie likes to say) when she has sent it through the Cash App.

Gardening is in my tool box, Binge watching Netflix with Dean, or spending time with my Great Pyrenees Lucy in the yard.

Giving to charity is in my toolbox, because I always feel better when I'm helping others. I give $21 a month to the USO because I believe in what they do. St. Labre Indian School about two times a year – for graduation in June and Christmas in December.

The children have learned to ask for help and that there is no shame in asking for help. They will reach out to one another and help wherever possible.

What does your toolbox look like? If you don't have one yet, now's the time to make it a priority. Everyone should have a toolbox.

Honoring our soldier this Fourth of July as he gets ready to deploy

Rachel, James, and Dean

Dean and grandson Cassius

L-R Maryann, Ursula, Dean, Sophia, James, Rachel, Izzy, Tom; Seated L-R Alejandra, Sydney

ia, James, and baby Cassius

Rose and James

MaryAnn, Rachel, James, Izzy, and Ursula

June 27, 2022

I woke up this morning in a sheer panic. I thought for sure Dean would hear my heart pounding so loudly as I lay in the bed next to him and so I quickly got up.

Tears are already streaming down my face as I make my way to the kitchen to start my coffee pot at the thought of James deploying at the end of July. Just a little more than 30 days and he's expected to be gone a whole year when you factor in the pre-deployment training and then the deployment itself to the Middle East.

Sophia had already made her way to the living room with grandson baby Cassius and so there was no being alone with my thoughts and being able to process them in solitude. I try to keep a brave face whenever possible, but this morning it was not going to happen as she immediately commented that i was up early. I had to share with her the truth that I'd woken in a sheer panic. Not that I don't have faith and complete trust in my son's ability to perform his duties as he serves his country and been trained but as a mom I turn to pure jello at the thought of him being even remote in harm's way. And I just have to allow myself to have that meltdown, and then allow time to slowly recover from it.

Sophia hasn't a clue what's in store for us but I have been through deployments in the past with Paul and Ray. It can be a very hard time, full of worry and sadness and loneliness. She purchased countdown blocks and has already started it. As of today we've got

434 days to go, that's including the times he will still be home. Lord help us, three hours later I feel like I can breathe again.

Today I will start a list and it's going to be a long list of all the things I'll get done in that time that James will be gone. It's called readying my toolbox. As a military mom it goes with the territory of having things to do to occupy your time and mind. Right now that the weather is beautiful it's time spent out in the yard and gardening. As the weather begins to turn cold I'll enjoy reading some books, and gathering things along with Sophia for care packages that get sent out almost immediately as soon as we have an address.

There's no doubt in my mind we will go through some rough spells, because a year is a long time to be without your spouse and Cassius will be 19 months by the time he sees his daddy again. But I'm just so grateful that Dean and I are in a position to be of help, to have James' little family in our home and we will get through this together... And as always one day at a time.

ABOUT THE AUTHOR

Rachel Clark is a wife and mother to six children and two step children. Rachel built Jeeps in Toledo, Ohio, for 33 years, and since retiring enjoys spending time watching the sunsets with her husband Dean Clark and faithful doggie companion, a Great Pyrenees named Lucy. Rachel finds peace in gardening and sells t-shirts on Etsy that she designs, sublimates, and tie-dyes herself. While her son is deployed with the United States Army, Rachel also helps care for her six month old grandson Cassius. Rachel has lived a sober life for 27 years.

You can find Rachel on the following socials:

YouTube - Retired Granny

Etsy - shopretiredgranny

Instagram - mrsrachel_clark

Facebook - How I Found My Peace

Special thanks to Heather Felty, publisher of Inner Peace Press, for her support and guidance in the creation of this book. If you are looking to make your book publishing dream a reality, check out Heather's writing coaching program, where she uses her unique ability of bringing out the best in your story to help you clarify your message. It was such a pleasure working with her!   www.innerpeacepress.com